Athlone French Poets

THÉOPHILE GAUTIER

Athlone French Poets

General Editor EILEEN LE BRETON

Reader in French Language and Literature,
Bedford College, University of London

MONOGRAPHS

Verlaine *by C. Chadwick*

Gérard de Nerval *by Norma Rinsler*

Saint-John Perse *by Roger Little*

Théophile Gautier *by P. E. Tennant*

CRITICAL EDITIONS

Paul Valéry: Charmes ou Poèmes
edited by Charles C. Whiting

Paul Verlaine: Sagesse
edited by C. Chadwick

Gérard de Nerval: Les Chimères
edited by Norma Rinsler

Saint-John Perse: Exil
edited by Roger Little

Théophile Gautier: Poésies
edited by Harry Cockerham

Alfred de Musset:
Contes d'Espagne et d'Italie
edited by Margaret A. Rees

Victor Hugo: Châtiments
edited by P. J. Yarrow

Théophile Gautier

by

P. E. TENNANT

UNIVERSITY OF LONDON

THE ATHLONE PRESS

1975

Published by
THE ATHLONE PRESS
UNIVERSITY OF LONDON
at 4 Gower Street, London WC1

Distributed by
Tiptree Book Services Ltd
Tiptree, Essex

U.S.A. and Canada
Humanities Press Inc
New Jersey

0 485 14604 5 *cloth*
0 485 12204 9 *paperback*

Printed in Great Britain by
The Garden City Press Limited
Letchworth, Hertfordshire
SG6 1JS

Athlone French Poets

General Editor EILEEN LE BRETON

This series is designed to provide students and general readers both with Monographs on important nineteenth- and twentieth-century French poets and Critical Editions of one or more representative works by these poets.

The Monographs aim at presenting the essential biographical facts while placing the poet in his social and intellectual context. They contain a detailed analysis of his poetical works and, where appropriate, a brief account of his other writings. His literary reputation is examined and his contribution to the development of French poetry is assessed, as is also his impact on other literatures. A selection of critical views and a bibliography are appended.

The critical Editions contain a substantial introduction aimed at presenting each work against its historical background as well as studying its genre, structure, themes, style, etc. and highlighting its relevance for today. The text normally given is the complete text of the original edition. It is followed by full commentaries on the poems and annotation of the text, including variant readings when these are of real significance.

E. Le B.

Le masque nous a rendus vrais

Gautier: 'Jean et Jeannette'

PREFACE

'. . . mal connu comme romancier, mal apprécié comme conteur de voyages et presque *inconnu* comme poète . . .': Baudelaire's evaluation of Gautier[1] seems as true today as it ever was. Already, within months of Gautier's death, Mallarmé asked significantly: 'Est-il, de ce destin, rien qui demeure?' ('Toast Funèbre'). Today, Gautier certainly remains one of the least read of all the great nineteenth-century French writers. Is the prediction of Emile Faguet in *Dix-Neuvième Siècle* already realized: 'Il périra, je crois, tout entier'? Yet it seems virtually axiomatic that such a total reversal of a once considerable reputation must be largely unjustified, and due as much to vagaries of fashion as to considered evaluation. If Gautier was overpraised by many of his contemporaries he is surely undervalued today. Of course, no service is rendered Gautier by making impossibly extravagant claims. It is grotesque to see him as the peer of Homer or Dante,[2] or as Bergerat's modern universal genius vying with Goethe for European supremacy.[3]

Nevertheless, the true nature of his purpose and achievement has not always been appreciated; as René Jasinski has pointed out in *Les Années Romantiques*, 'le véritable Gautier échappe en général à tout ce qui l'a fait blâmer ou célébrer' (*AR* 125). The misunderstanding has indeed appeared at times despairingly total, almost perverse. Even the respected Edmund Wilson can write astonishingly that Gautier and the Parnassians 'seemed to have taken it for their aim merely to picture historical incidents and natural phenomena as objectively and accurately as possible in impassive, perfect verse'.[4] Well might Jasinski exclaim in a similar context, 'on croit rêver!' (*AR* 124).

After Gautier's death the cultural climate long remained generally alien to his aesthetic, and although modern taste now accepts patently decorative as well as conceptual art it still seems unlikely that any dramatic swing to reinstate the poet to his former eminence will occur in the foreseeable future. What academic interest Gautier has provoked in recent years has mostly been directed to specialised aspects of his fiction. Even this author's sheer cumulative achievement has never been fully recognized, but to the modern mind, easily suspicious of prodigality, even this is a dubious virtue.

Yet it is undeniable, as the present work attempts to show—without aiming specifically to 'rehabilitate' Gautier—that his work possesses intrinsic as well as historical value, that his range was not as narrow as is often thought, and that beneath the mask of imperturbability lay a deep and aggrieved humanity. The present introduction to Gautier therefore aims, by considering sympathetically some of the major aspects of his poetry and prose, to challenge some assumptions as well as to convey basic information, and to suggest that 'le bon Théo' was more than a mere word-spinner.

Like his brilliant conversation, his work is rich in paradox and ambiguity. Poised between Northern and Mediterranean cultures, 'fils de la Grèce antique et de la jeune France',[5] Gautier attempted to embrace ultimately irreconcilable elements of cosmopolitan culture in one harmonious ideal of beauty. Loving the principle of beauty in all things, he believed that the work of art was man's supreme achievement, and that its pursuit enables him to transcend himself and his condition. Life for him was squalid because it was imperfect, constantly tempting man to submerge his unlimited potential in a grubbing materialism. It is this message, with its many ramifications of deep, perennial consequence to humanity, which illuminates the whole of Gautier's work.

'One is a fool, of course, if one forego the pleasure of Gautier', remarked Ezra Pound in 'The Renaissance'. To read Gautier is ultimately rewarding and challenging as well as merely pleasing.

London, 1974   P. T.

CONTENTS

ABBREVIATIONS

I

LIFE

Gautier's life (1811–72)[1] spans a major part of the nineteenth century, a period in France not only of unparalleled intellectual and artistic creativity but of intense political and social ferment. The poet's roots reach back into a now utterly remote pre-industrial culture, while at his death the France of the Third Republic was already assuming the characteristic features of the modern industrial state. Yet priding himself on being essentially 'romantique de naissance',[2] Gautier consistently chose to condemn or ignore the new dynamic forces shaping his country's destiny.

Théophile Gautier was born on 30 August 1811 at Tarbes, within sight of the Pyrenees. His father was a fairly cultured minor civil servant whose family had been established in the Midi for several generations. His mother's family were in the service of the influential Montesquiou family of Mauperthuis, 50 kms. east of Paris. The Montesquious also possessed property at Artagnan, near Tarbes, and it was in the Château d'Artagnan, later to be celebrated by Dumas, that Gautier's parents probably met, were married and lived for a while before settling in Tarbes.

In the conservative reaction after Napoleon's abdication in 1814, Gautier's father found promotion through his connection with the Abbé de Montesquiou, then Minister of the Interior. The family accordingly moved to Paris, settling in the ancient Marais district, where the young Gautier soon became, as he confessed, 'quoique né sur les frontières de l'Espagne . . . un Parisien complet, badaud, flâneur' ('Préface', *Les Jeunes-France*).

Gautier's schooldays (1822–9) were unremarkable as such, except that under his father's excellent tuition he became a good Latin scholar, revealing however a preference then considered unhealthy for 'decadent' authors like Martial and Claudian and, he claimed, for equally unwholesome French writers like Villon and Rabelais—tastes which he was never to disavow. At the same time he already displayed significant artistic aptitudes, as his son-in-law Emile Bergerat later recorded:

Le temps des récréations était invariablement consacré à dessiner et à peindre, et toute sa famille croyait à cette époque que Théophile serait peintre (*EB* 40).

While at school he formed an enduring friendship with the slightly older Gérard de Nerval, already successful as a writer and to whom Gautier came to owe much.[3] From about 1826 onwards Gautier began composing poetry, and many of these earliest pieces were included in the collection *Poésies*, published in 1830.

Meanwhile, the long school vacations were spent at Mauperthuis on the Montesquious' estate, where Gautier's aunt was married to the bailiff, and the dreamy beauty of this Ile-de-France landscape, associated with a shadowy adolescent love affair, was transposed a few years later in the introspective, pastoral idylls evoked in *Poésies* and the novel *Mademoiselle de Maupin*. In one vacation (1825), the fourteen-year-old schoolboy undertook the restoration of the village church's paintings and decorated the nave with a large Biblical scene.

The last two years of Gautier's schooldays proved crucial in this formative period. Increasingly he felt torn between two equally attractive vocations: 'placé à l'Y du carrefour, nous hésitions entre les deux routes, c'est-à-dire entre la poésie et la peinture' (*SR* 26).[4] In 1829 he began to frequent the nearby studio of the painter Louis-Edouard Rioult, and in later life often regretted not having followed this early vocation—though it seems doubtful from surviving paintings whether his talent was more than technical competence.[5] The call of literature was even more insistent, and here, paradoxically, the studio itself encouraged his poetic vocation. Artists were then almost as preoccupied with literature as with painting, as Gautier himself records: 'On lisait beaucoup alors dans les ateliers. Les rapins aimaient les lettres . . .' (*HR* 4). In all the arts, the ferment of new ideas and bold techniques, the urge to experiment, to widen horizons, were beginning to crystallise into a recognisable movement. The whole cultural climate was heady with revolutionary romanticism which the boy Gautier found irresistible:

Les générations actuelles doivent se figurer difficilement l'effervescence des esprits à cette époque; il s'opérait un mouvement pareil à celui de la Renaissance. Une sève de vie nouvelle circulait impétueusement. Tout germait, tout bourgeonnait, tout éclatait à la fois. Des parfums vertigineux se dégageaient des fleurs; l'air grisait, on était fou de lyrisme et d'art. Il semblait qu'on vînt de retrouver le grand secret perdu, et cela était vrai, on avait retrouvé la poésie (*HR* 2).

The quickening tempo reached a climax in February 1830, when the legendary *première* of Hugo's archetypal romantic drama *Hernani*, unforgettably evoked by Gautier in his *Histoire du Romantisme* and to whose triumph Gautier had greatly contributed, presented a milestone in Gautier's life. As Hugo's 'plus fanatique séide' (*SR* 207), Gautier ordered a provocative waistcoat to celebrate the occasion[6] and increasingly abandoned Rioult's studio: 'peu à peu je négligeai la peinture et me tournai vers les idées littéraires' (*SR* 9).

The result was that on 28 July 1830 Gautier published, at his father's expense, his first volume of poetry, *Poésies*, a modest collection of forty-two short pieces composed over the last few years, reflecting various facets of fashionable adolescent attitudes but displaying nevertheless a promising technical competence and some individuality of treatment. But simultaneously the uneasy political peace was shattered by the 1830 July uprising, and Gautier's first poems were left unsold: 'le vent ne souffle pas à la poésie', he lamented ('Préface', *Albertus*)—a complaint he was to echo several times later in his life. For many young romantics the aftermath of the 1830 Revolution was a period of intense disillusionment, and Gautier bemoaned in a series of pessimistic poems composed at this time the tastelessness and mediocrity of a period he felt to be increasingly alien to the artist, reserving his greatest scorn for politics.[7]

Towards the end of 1831 therefore Gautier and his friends gathered round the person of a young sculptor, Jean Duseigneur, to form the Petit Cénacle, a more ostentatious version of Hugo's Cénacle and grouping together the more irresponsible of Hugo's young disciples.[8] The Petit Cénacle clique soon gained a reputation for extravagance, oddity and bourgeois-baiting, *Le Figaro* coining the term 'Jeunes-France' in amused contempt of its members; but it was important as a refuge from a society apparently preoccupied with material gain and as constituting the first recognisable cradle of ideas later to become known as Art for

Art's Sake. The colourful legend of the exuberant, irresponsible Gautier, with waist-length hair and perpetually sporting the impertinent *Hernani* waistcoat, dates from this time. The truth appears somewhat different, however: while enjoying this congenial buffoonery Gautier retained a lucid detachment from its lunatic fringe. He proved his independence by satirising the group's excesses in a long narrative poem, 'Albertus', a complex mosaic of romantic themes set in a climate of mock-heroic satanism, which was incorporated along with twenty more short poems and an important 'Préface,' in a new, enlarged edition of *Poésies* in 1832. The Petit Cénacle phase was further reflected in a series of short stories collected in 1833 as *Les Jeunes-France*, defined by the author as an 'espèce de Précieuses ridicules du romantisme' (*SR* 9), and flippantly indebted to the now fashionable E. T. A. Hoffmann.

In September 1833 Gautier signed a contract for a novel, *Mademoiselle de Maupin*, and in December for a series of twelve monthly articles aimed at 'exhuming' neglected French writers of the past; these essays were later grouped to form *Les Grotesques*, published in 1844. The first of them, devoted to Villon, appeared in *La France Littéraire* early in 1834, causing great controversy. An anonymous critic in *Le Constitutionnel*, a semi-official newspaper already mentioned disparagingly by Gautier in *Les Jeunes-France*, attacked Gautier for condoning immorality in his articles on Villon and Théophile de Viau. A legal battle ensued in which Gautier's articles were cleared of the charge—an episode significant as being the first major legal case of the century involving an attempt at literary censorship on moral, as opposed to political, grounds. Undeterred however, Gautier composed a truculent counterblast to conservatism in his celebrated 'Préface' to *Mademoiselle de Maupin* (1834), a veritable manifesto of Art for Art's Sake doctrine.

Meanwhile, Gautier's father had suffered financially in the 1830 Revolution, and when the family moved to a more modest house on the outskirts of Paris the poet decided to remain in the city, settling about October 1834 with Nerval and other bohemian friends in the picturesque backwater of the dilapidated Doyenné district.[9] Here, as 'la Bohème du Doyenné', the young aesthetes lived for a while in the gallant attic style Murger and—much later, in an adulterated version—Puccini were to popularise:

Nous menions alors une vie sauvage et truculente dans cette impasse du Doyenné . . . vêtu d'habits impossibles, les épaules inondées, comme par une crinière de lion, d'une chevelure plus que mérovingienne . . . (*SR* 207).

Life in the Doyenné community was enlivened with a series of costumed balls and one of these, probably held in November 1835 to celebrate the success of the first volume of *Mademoiselle de Maupin*, was particularly spectacular, involving elaborate rococo decorations largely improvised by the artists themselves.[10] The novel *Mademoiselle de Maupin*, a crucial text for the study of romantic yearning and disillusion but immediately notorious for its ambiguous morality, was Gautier's first moderate financial success and established his lifelong reputation for the scandalous.

Since 1831 Gautier had been contributing articles intermittently to various journals, and through the intervention of Balzac who had just founded *La Revue de Paris* he now embarked (August 1836) on the regular journalistic career which was to weigh on him so heavily for the remainder of his days. Journalism provided Gautier with a reasonably secure livelihood, besides offering him unique opportunities for foreign travel and above all for making influential contacts in high society and the world of the arts. Gautier himself, however, convinced that potential artistic genius was being prostituted for ephemeral hack-work, never forgave the hated *feuilleton* for depriving him of his liberty and for creating in him a permanent complex of frustration and guilt. 'Le livre seul a de l'importance et de la durée', he pointedly remarked: 'le journal disparaît et s'oublie' (M. du Camp, *Théophile Gautier*, p. 53).

After a brief tour of Belgium and Holland with Nerval in 1836, serialisation of the 'roman incroyable' 'Fortunio', 'un hymne à la beauté, à la richesse, au bonheur' ('Préface'), followed in 1837. This was succeeded by a series of delightfully escapist short stories, collected later as *Nouvelles* (1845), and by his début as dramatist with the charming *Une Larme du Diable* (1839). Meanwhile, Gautier was now composing poetry continuously and in 1838 published *La Comédie de la Mort*, grouping together many miscellaneous pieces from the exhilarating Jeunes-France years and culminating in the sombre title-poem. This varied volume reflects for the first time Gautier's mature poetic talent.

Looking back nostalgically in later years, it seemed to Gautier that his nonchalant youthful period was coming to an end at this time, a break painfully underscored by his increasing journalistic commitments. 'Là finit ma vie heureuse, indépendante et prime-sautière', he recorded (*SR* 11), and in *La Comédie de la Mort*, apart from the heavily romantic despair of the title-poem, a major cycle of bitterly despondent poems stresses a persistent note of dejection at this time.

A major emotional revelation followed in 1840, however, when Gautier spent five crowded summer months touring a Spain still largely unknown with a wealthy dilettante friend from the Doyenné, Eugène Piot. The immediate literary results of this voyage of discovery were recorded in the exuberant *Voyage en Espagne* (1843), arguably Gautier's finest travelogue, and a corresponding series of poems collected together as *España* in 1845. Gautier claimed that this journey gave him an insatiable thirst to travel: 'Depuis, je n'eus d'autre idée que de ramasser quelque somme et de partir: la passion ou la maladie du voyage s'était développée en moi' (*SR* 12).

The Parisian life to which the traveller reluctantly returned was more crowded than ever. In addition to preparing his travel impressions for publication and resuming his regular journalism, Gautier dashed off the scenario for a romantic ballet, *Giselle*, based on a picturesque legend retold by his friend Heine. The ballet achieved instant success in June 1841 through Adolphe Adam's music and the art of its star interpreter, the rising ballerina Carlotta Grisi, soon to attract large audiences in London, Berlin and Moscow as well as in Paris. The association between Gautier and the world of dance remained close from this time; he composed many other ballets (notably *La Péri*, 1843, *Pâquerette*, 1851, and *Gemma*, 1854), sometimes travelling abroad to supervise foreign productions. Gautier was emotionally involved too; his platonic relationship with the dancer Carlotta inspired several exquisite poems, besides the poignant novel *Spirite* (1865–6). The poet was obliged, however, to substitute for the ethereal Carlotta her more practical sister, the operatic contralto Ernesta Grisi, with whom in 1844 he set up a semi-permanent *ménage*, having by her two daughters, Judith and Estelle. Gautier had now made the acquaintance of the young Baudelaire and of the celebrated demi-mondaine Madame Sabatier, probably in 1843, and he became a regular and welcome visitor to the latter's salon in Montmartre, savouring there the company of Musset, Baudelaire, Flaubert, Dumas and others. His occasional experiments with fashionable drug-taking at this time are recounted vividly in 'Le Club des Haschischins' (1846).

Other literary successes came in these productive years: a comedy or two inspired by the *Commedia dell'Arte* against the prevailingly bourgeois theatrical fashion (*Le Tricorne Enchanté*, 1845, *Pierrot Posthume*, 1847), a variety of short stories and, especially, the honour of an edition of *Poésies Complètes* in 1845. Retrospectively this period appears astonishingly successful for Gautier: recognised officially as 'homme de lettres' in his nomination as Chevalier de la Légion d'Honneur in 1842, established as an influential critic, attending court galas at Versailles and cherishing the constant stimulus of his friendship with Nerval, Balzac, Banville, Baudelaire and Hugo. Relatively prosperous and elegant, he took childish delight in the possession of a pony and trap.

The year of the 1848 Revolution brutally interrupted this period. The Revolution itself, closing theatres and disrupting artistic life generally, drastically reduced Gautier's income. Moreover, this disaster was followed immediately by the death of his mother in March, an event which moved the poet deeply, inspiring the bitter lines of 'Le Glas Intérieur' (*DP*). As life resumed after the Revolution the poet's journalistic commitments, and the time-consuming visits to theatres and exhibitions which these involved, were now more onerous than ever. His mother's funeral expenses were paid for by a *feuilleton* in *La Presse* the following day,[11] and between April and December 1848, it has been calculated,[12] almost one hundred articles, constituting the equivalent of four solid books, were written. In spite of this incessant toil, however, Gautier continued to write poetry as a safety valve: 'on fait de la prose pour les autres et des vers pour soi'.[13] The various pieces that were to compose *Emaux et Camées* were being prepared by the dejected poet, disappointed along with so many others that the Revolution had not brought the hoped-for revival of a new artistic climate.

In 1850 a first voyage to Italy, culminating in a prolonged stay in Venice, one of his 'patries idéales' (*VI* 65), fulfilled a long-cherished dream, and in June 1852 Gautier embarked on another journey abroad, visiting this time Malta, Smyrna and Constantinople and returning via Athens, where he eloquently recorded the sublimity of classical architecture:

Athènes m'a transporté. A côté du Parthénon, tout semble barbare et grossier . . . la peinture moderne n'est qu'un tatouage de cannibale et la statuaire un pétrissage de magots difformes. Revenant d'Athènes, Venise m'a paru triviale et grotesquement décadente (*EB* 295).

Later he confirmed 'la vue du Parthénon m'a guéri de la maladie gothique' (*SR* 13).

It was during this absence abroad that the first edition of Gautier's most celebrated volume of poetry, *Emaux et Camées*, was published (17 July 1852), bringing the poet universal acclaim though little actual revenue. Although the former romantic is still much in evidence in this volume, which is far from being the coldly impersonal collection sometimes alleged, *Emaux et Camées*, appearing almost simultaneously with Leconte de Lisle's *Poèmes Antiques*, does appear to mark a significant turning point in the history of French poetry. The volume underlines the clear evolution in the literary climate away from overtly lyrical genres towards a more aesthetic and objective manner which proclaims the pre-eminence of art over 'life'.

Gautier had now arrived at a prominent position in the literary world. With Chateaubriand dead, Lamartine, Vigny and Musset in virtual retirement, and Hugo in exile, he was now unchallenged as sole survivor of the heroic days of romanticism. His prestige was confirmed by his directing for several years (1851–6) the authoritative *Revue de Paris*.

Meanwhile, publication of *Italia* (later to become *Voyage en Italie*) and *Constantinople* followed in 1852 and 1853, reviewing enthusiastically his recent visits to Italy and the Middle East. Further novels appeared and were well received. Yet for all the acclaim, these years had an aimless, dispiriting character. Twice, seeking a sinecure as refuge from unremitting journalism, Gautier solicited in vain the post of Inspector of Fine Arts for which he was so well suited. He was also involved in a protracted legal battle with the publisher Buloz over the non-appearance of the long-promised novel, *Le Capitaine Fracasse*. The première of Verdi's opera *Ernani* in 1854, based on Hugo's drama, reawoke nostalgia for the raptures of now far-off days. Then successive deaths, those of his father, of his generous friend the charming Madame de Girardin, and the tragic suicide of his friend Nerval, came as sombre reminders of mortality to the author of 'La Comédie de la Mort'. Movingly he wrote:

... voir disparaître les chers cercueils sous la terre brune, enfouir soi-même les têtes aimées, pleurer ses espérances à jamais perdues, sentir diminuer jour par jour le trésor de sa jeunesse, cela est tout simple et tout naturel.[14]

In 1855 Gautier left *La Presse* for the semi-official *Le Moniteur Universel*, but the routine burden of regular journalism continued as crushing as ever. Nevertheless, in 1856 he took over the influential review *L'Artiste*, sharing the editorship with an old Doyenné friend Arsène Houssaye and disseminating Art for Art's Sake doctrines through many editorials. 1857 saw the publication of more fiction, including the astonishingly documented *Le Roman de la Momie*, reconstructing the civilisation of Ancient Egypt. In 1857 too came the flattering dedication of Baudelaire's *Les Fleurs du Mal*, 'au Poète Impeccable, au Parfait Magicien ès Lettres Françaises', crowning many years of mutual esteem between the two poets; while Gautier's friendship with Banville provoked his celebrated statement of Parnassian principles, the poem 'L'Art', incorporated into later editions of *Emaux et Camées*.

In autumn 1858 Gautier left with semi-official encouragement for an extended visit to Russia, in order to gather material for a monumental volume, *Trésors d'Art de la Russie*. However, the project failed commercially through lack of subscribers, leaving a residue of articles subsequently rearranged to form the delightful 'livre neigeux et brumeux',[15] *Voyage en Russie* (1867). The same year, the massive compilation *L'Histoire de l'Art Dramatique en France depuis Vingt-Cinq Ans* appeared, comprising Gautier's collected theatre reviews for the years 1837–52. Yet in spite of everything, Gautier seemed increasingly discouraged—witness the moving letter to his sisters composed in a snow-bound St Petersburg.

The last twelve years of Gautier's life are a record of uninterrupted writing punctuated by further travels abroad: Algeria, Italy once more, and his only visit to Egypt, in 1869, as member of the official delegation to the inauguration of the Suez Canal. Although rejected by the French Academy three times (1867, 1868, 1869), these are years of assured literary fame. In 1863 Sainte-Beuve, the most influential critic of the day, set the seal of approval on the poet by devoting no less than three major articles to a review of Gautier's entire published work.[16] The long-delayed picaresque cloak-and-dagger novel *Le Capitaine Fracasse* finally began serialisation in 1861, provoking wide acclaim and winning for the chronically impecunious writer a much-needed state pension. The luminous short novel *Spirite* followed in 1865, poignantly evoking Gautier's love for Carlotta Grisi.

These years are the brash, brilliant heyday of the Second Empire, an age of ostentatious material success associated with the rise of commercial power and culminating in the Exposition Universelle of 1867. Along with many other embittered artists, Gautier felt that no age, not even the previous drab monarchy, was less congenial to the aesthete: 'L'esprit, en proie à d'autres préoccupations et tourné vers les recherches scientifiques et historiques, s'est détourné de la poésie', he records (*HR* 358), concluding bitterly: 'Chanter pour les sourds est une mélancolique occupation'. In spite of his acceptance in 1866 of an official commission to undertake a survey of recent poetry for the Exhibition year—resulting in the *Progrès de la Poésie française*, incorporated in the *Histoire du Romantisme*—Gautier's private life begins increasingly to appear a deliberate insulation from the new climate of realism in art. More than ever he cherished his social contacts, shining still in Madame Sabatier's salon and at the celebrated Magny dinners inaugurated in 1862.

In 1865 Gautier was admitted to the fashionable salon of the generous Princess Mathilde, cousin of Napoleon III and niece to Bonaparte, and at these receptions came quickly, through his engaging personality and the verve of his conversation, to occupy a prominent, even favoured position among the many eminent guests. Bergerat records:

Théophile Gautier tenait le haut bout de la table chez la princesse Mathilde. Il était le charme de ses réunions et l'attrait de ses fêtes. Jamais il ne fut plus étincelant de verve que dans cette maison où il se sentait heureux, entouré d'admirateurs sympathiques et d'amis (*EB* 17).

Gautier immensely enjoyed this 'amitié voluptueuse',[17] and when in 1868 the Princess offered him a sinecure as her librarian, he repaid her kindness with boundless gratitude, recorded in the poetic homage of an exquisite sonnet sequence (*Un Douzain de Sonnets*, *DP*). Through the Princess he had access to the court of Napoleon III.[18]

Yet an underlying sense of disillusion and bitterness is evident in these years, as a letter to his daughter Estelle in September 1866 eloquently testifies: 'Ennuie-toi, il le faut bien; l'ennui est le fond de l'étoffe, mais on y peut broder quelques fleurs d'imagination'. Frequent residence at St Gratien, Princess Mathilde's country estate, and visits to Carlotta at her home near Geneva provided temporary consolation, but 'le bon Théo' had become 'le pauvre Théo', a self-confessed anachronism who had outlived his times: 'Pour moi, il me semble que je ne suis plus un contemporain ... Je parlerais volontiers de mon individu à la troisième personne ... J'ai comme le sentiment de n'être déjà plus vivant'.[19]

Brusquely all was shattered by the dramatic events of the Franco-Prussian war. In September 1870 Gautier hurriedly returned from Carlotta's to Paris on hearing of the Prussian advance on the capital. The ageing poet remained with his family in Paris throughout the invasion and the aftermath of the Commune, enduring great privation and distress. As all cultural life was suspended Gautier substituted for his usual reviews a series of graphic sketches of the war-stricken city which composed later the moving *Tableaux de Siège* (1872). The triumphant return of Hugo from exile, following the defeat of Napoleon III, was the one luminous event in the gloom: 'Causer de poésie avec Hugo', he remarked to Bergerat after the reunion of the two poets, 'c'est causer de divinité avec le bon Dieu' (*EB* 93).

Later, his intimates saw the events of 1870–1 as directly responsible for Gautier's end, and the morose Gautier himself anticipated their verdict: 'Cette révolution, c'est ma fin . . . Vous pensez bien que, maintenant, je ne puis plus recommencer à faire ma vie.'[20] Long-standing cardiac disease, aggravated by recent near-destitution, advanced rapidly and the poet died on 23 October 1872, aged sixty-two. The poet's last lines were devoted to a nostalgic evocation of the première of *Hernani*. One of the last visitors was Banville, with whom the dying Gautier talked serenely of art. His friend the painter Hébert wrote to the deeply-moved Princess Mathilde: 'Qui pourra jamais dire ce qu'était Théo comme hauteur de pensée et comme grâce d'esprit?'

II

AESTHETIC DOCTRINE

Gautier evolved no systematic or totally consistent aesthetic doctrine: he was an exuberant and temperamental artist, not a logical thinker or 'intellectual' in the sense that Vigny, Mallarmé, or Valéry could be said to be. Indeed, it has been claimed that 'Gautier n'est nullement un esthéticien'.[1] The word 'doctrine' is inapplicable in the strict sense, and, moreover, Gautier's poetic practice does not necessarily conform to his theoretical views—as any attempt to correlate the principles enumerated in 'L'Art' with the contents of *Emaux et Camées* shows. On certain broad principles, however, Gautier was consistent, and he constantly returns to discuss these in his work irrespective of context.

Gautier's temperament was assimilative; his views are far from original, and they are extremely eclectic. In particular he owes major debts to Aristotle, Plato, Ronsard and the Pléiade, to the general *précieux* tradition, to eighteenth-century (particularly German) aesthetics and, of course, to the diffuse experience known as Romanticism. Perhaps wisely, the poet never attempted a synthesis of his artistic convictions, and these are consequently scattered at random throughout a work of daunting volume. What follows is an attempt to abstract the broad lines of the doctrine which may serve as introduction to a subject of greater complexity than has often been thought.

THE DIVINITY OF ART

Like most poets Gautier was unable to reach a satisfactory definition of either poetry itself or its ultimate object, 'le type de la beauté à l'état idéal',[2] or absolute beauty. He holds a continual dialogue with himself in an attempt to reach a clear perception of this absolute, visualised in a variety of ways. At times it appears as a preconceived or innate ideal[3] of which the artist is allowed an intuitive apprehension through the medium of its sensuous form, material beauty. At other times this absolute is imagined as a glimpse of some former state,[4] now irretrievable, but towards which the poet nevertheless gropes in his effort to be reintegrated with the soul's 'patrie',[5] movingly described in 'Pensée de Minuit' (*CM*).

Yet another expression of the same concept is the notion, taken from Goethe, of the 'microcosm', defined by Gautier as 'un petit monde complet d'où il [l'artiste] tire la pensée et la forme de ses œuvres', or 'cette précieuse faculté d'une création intérieure'.[6] But however the notion of the ideal be expressed, it is certain that for Gautier, as for Baudelaire, the essence of reality is not material but spiritual, and that it is this fundamental spirituality which feeds the artist's imagination.

Following Plato and, more immediately, eighteenth-century German aestheticians, this pure, absolute beauty is assimilated to truth: 'le beau est la splendeur du vrai'.[7] The various embodiments of this absolute—classic and gothic, ancient and modern, harmony and virtuosity, camellia and daisy—are shifting, tantalising and equally irresistible symbols: 'J'ai usé ma vie à poursuivre, pour le dépeindre, le Beau sous toutes ses formes de Protée', proclaims Gautier (*EB* 128). The artist is particularly aware of 'le beau de chaque époque et de chaque contrée' (*A* LXXVI), Baudelaire noting of Gautier that 'son esprit est un miroir cosmopolite de beauté'.[8] The artist's task is to endow these relative forms with the stamp and essence of ideal beauty. For Gautier as for Baudelaire beauty thus comprises a duality of an eternal, immutable element and a transitory, relative one.[9]

One convenient way of expressing the concept of absolute beauty is to identify it with God: 'le beau dans son essence absolue, c'est Dieu';[10] and *Mademoiselle de Maupin* especially includes many a rhapsody to beauty as 'la Divinité visible' (*MM* 149). Consequently the poet becomes a member of a priesthood dedicated to 'la religion de la beauté',[11] potentially 'le rival et l'égal de Dieu' or even indistinguishable from God himself: 'le poète absolu ... serait aussi grand que Dieu'.[12] Indeed, the true artist's sublimity places him even higher:

Dites! Est-il un philosophe, un conquérant, un législateur, un prophète, Dieu même, qui ait fait autant pour l'humanité que Virgile et que Raphael?[13]

The fervour of Gautier's personal stance is striking: 'Nous

avons cru, nous avons aimé, nous avons admiré, nous avons eu la sublime folie de l'art';[14] and Baudelaire stresses this fixation: 'le goût du Beau est pour [Gautier] un *fatum* parce qu'il a fait de son devoir une *idée* fixe' (*BOC* 689). Gautier's fervent aestheticism elevates art into a substitute for true religious experience.

The poet in his worship of beauty is saintly or monk-like, 'noble créature',[15] 'désintéressé',[16] inevitably withdrawn. Poets 's'exercent dans le silence, l'ombre et la solitude, comme ces pianistes qui la nuit travaillent à se délier les doigts sur des claviers muets pour ne pas importuner leurs voisins' (*HR* 358). Equally characteristic of the true artist, however, are the wilder features of the elevated emotional state traditionally associated with the romantic concept of inspiration—rapture, ecstasy, 'ivresse'—and Gautier subscribes to the traditional view, recently revived by the romantics via the Pléiade and the eighteenth-century concept of 'enthusiasm', of the poet as a possessed, frenzied spirit, symbolised by his recurrent image of the 'poète échevelé' astride his unmanageable hippogryph.[17] Far from soothing, art consumes with a unique intensity: 'la passion du beau nous tient et nous tourmente'.[18]

Socially, such uniqueness inevitably becomes a curse, 'un don fatal, une sorte de malédiction' (*HR* 160), making the artist an eccentric, derisory figure alienated from the workaday world, but for which moments of sublimity unkown to the prosaic majority amply compensate.[19] There is, moreover, an inherent personal danger in this isolation: a progressive narcissism may render the artist subject to hallucination and ultimate madness. Clearly, therefore, the poet is essentially different from the rest of men. He is, in fact, a member of a privileged minority, and it follows that poetry as an act is not primarily a shared, public experience but a private diversion, for 'chaque poète a sa lyre et chante seul' (*HR* 305). The hallmark of the artist is the possession of a private vision: 'Tout homme qui n'a pas son monde à traduire n'est pas un artiste'.[20]

The way is clearly open for an arrogantly aristocratic, elitist view of art: 'la poésie, la musique et la peinture . . . ne se livrent qu'à certaines organisations d'élite'.[21] Poetry, being intimate, easily tends to the esoteric; it is 'cette admirable langue que le monde entend et ne parle pas' (*HR* 301). Consequently the artist,

contemptuous of the uninitiated 'troupeau vil',[22] ceases to preoccupy himself with communication; and while this haughty
dismissal of 'la foule'[23] and 'le suffrage des imbéciles'[24] does not
result, in Gautier's case, in the hermeticism of a Donne or a
Mallarmé, he approves of making no concessions to the public:
'Ne fais pas d'escalier à ta pensée ardue',[25] he counsels, confessing
that

Pour notre compte, nous aimons assez l'art hiéroglyphique, escarpé, où
l'on n'entre pas chez soi; il faut relever la foule jusqu'à l'œuvre, et non
rabaisser l'œuvre jusqu'à la foule.[26]

Gautier is adamant that the artist's peculiar character is a
divine gift; poetry is 'une chose de tempérament; on naît poète
comme on naît blond ou brun';[27] for

En toute chose, il ne faut jamais méconnaître le don, qui est dans les
arts comme la grâce en religion. Dieu l'accorde à qui il veut, et les
mérites n'y font rien; ni le travail, ni la volonté, ni l'intelligence, ni l'art
ne peuvent suppléer le don; beaucoup de talent ne remplace jamais une
étincelle de génie, et toute l'application du monde est inefficace sans la
disposition . . . la vieille maxime du poète est toujours vraie: 'Nascitur,
non fit'. [28]

The creative urge, as opposed to the creative act, lies beyond the
will and, even in the happy few, operates only intermittently:

La poésie n'est pas un état permanent de l'âme. Les mieux doués ne
sont visités par le dieu que de loin en loin; la volonté n'y peut rien . . .
Seul parmi les ouvriers de l'art, le poète ne saurait être laborieux, son
travail ne dépend pas de lui.[29]

Inspiration is a capricious cherub,[30] 'une bouche invisible [qui
vous] souffle à l'oreille'[31] or, in the most striking metaphor, a
kind of cosmic or solar emanation to which the poet is attuned:
'Soyons traversés, comme des prismes, par les rayons des soleils
et les effluves des univers!'[32]

The cult of pure, unalloyed beauty means that art inescapably
possesses moral value;[33] the aesthetic ideal merges into a moral
one, and 'ce qui est beau physiquement est bien, tout ce qui est
laid est mal' (*MM* 210). Offering that 'plaisir supérieur qui
détache de la grossière réalité',[34] art involves a process of refinement, a striving for perfection and distinction in the world of the

grisâtre. For Gautier, the purpose of art is clear: 'élever l'homme'.[35] The corollary is that art is a refuge and a compensation for life, 'ce qui console le mieux de vivre' ('Préface,' *Albertus*). An element of revolt is therefore implicit: the poet-artist not only rejects the mediocrity of existence (his verse is often elegiac, recording as it does the gap between dream and reality) but the very condition of mortality. For Gautier as for many of the romantics, art is essentially the attempt to escape from exile and to recapture possession of an ideal former state, 'remonter à la cause première' ('L'Oiseau Captif', *P*).

All this does not mean, however, that art must necessarily be solemn or pretentious, like that of 'les talents soporifiques'[36] in the deadpan Malherbian tradition at which Gautier scoffs. An essential quality of the true artist is fancy, and this wayward component, variously called 'fantaisie', 'chimère', 'caprice', enables the artist to stumble on truth accidentally, as it were. Gautier defines the 'chimère' significantly as 'quelque chose d'inutile, espèce de desideratum de l'infini, de vague aspiration à l'idéal, de souvenir inconscient d'un état antérieur',[37] and the apparent frivolity of poets is therefore illusory: 'leur moindre fantaisie est une œuvre éternelle' ('Compensation', *CM*).

The most striking illustration of this apparent inconsequentiality is the doctrine of correspondences, pinpointed by Gautier in his key essay on Baudelaire, and defined by him as the capacity to discover

... par une intuition secrète des rapports invisibles à d'autres et rapprocher ainsi, par des analogies inattendues que seul le *voyant* peut saisir, les objets les plus éloignés et les plus opposés en apparence. Tout vrai poète est doué de cette qualité plus ou moins développée, qui est l'essence de son art.[38]

Such a faculty demands that the artist be idle, socially superfluous, and the narcissistic dreamer of *Poésies*, of the Preface to *Albertus*, of the poem 'A un Jeune Tribun' (*CM*) reminds the reader that art is the preserve of the dilettante: 'L'art, c'est la liberté, le luxe, l'efflorescence, c'est l'épanouissement de l'âme dans l'oisiveté' ('Préface', *Albertus*). These views derive fundamentally from the concept of art as play associated with Kant and his disciples, which had become common coinage in generalised form in the circles in which Gautier moved (see below, p. 126, n. 40). According to this view, art is valuable in proportion as it is disinterested, frivolous; when it becomes 'pure' it ceases to be solemn. Apparent flippancy may well be reconciled with an underlying seriousness of intent; and Gautier's comment on Watteau, that 'son art est sérieux, même si ses sujets semblent frivoles', [39] would apply to his own art.

One result is that Gautier reveres most those artists gifted with a kind of nonchalant charm, like Nerval's 'naiveté enjouée' (*HR* 140) or La Fontaine's 'bonhomie rêveuse' (*HR* 383), and this quality is especially impressive when allied to prodigality, as in the Banville of the *Odes Funambulesques*:

Jamais la fantaisie ne se livra à un plus joyeux gaspillage de richesses . . . cette spirituelle débauche poétique . . . est peut-être son œuvre la plus originale. Nous croyons qu'on peut admettre dans la poésie ces caprices bouffons comme on admet les arabesques en peinture (*HR* 305).

The provocative stance adopted by Gautier in the Preface to *Les Jeunes-France* ('en fait d'artistes, je n'estime que les acrobates') is no doubt not totally serious; but it is nevertheless towards the type of art symbolised in Banville's 'Saut du Tremplin' that he looks for the ultimate expression of the artistic spirit in its ascension towards the ideal.

THE AUTONOMY OF ART

All the foregoing implies that the artist has, in effect, a kind of divine right to create a work of pure art without reference to extraneous considerations of any kind—a position well illustrated by Gautier's statement of editorial policy in his review *L'Artiste* on 14 December 1856:

Nous apportons donc à *L'Artiste* la passion de l'art,—nous pourrions même dire son dilettantisme et sa volupté. Nous croyons à l'autonomie de l'Art; l'Art pour nous n'est pas le moyen mais le but; tout artiste qui se propose autre chose que le beau n'est pas un artiste à nos yeux.

German eighteenth century aesthetics directly prepared the ground for the *l'art pour l'art* debate in France,[40] while historically, it has been argued,[41] Art for Art's Sake has often been associated

with periods when, as in the France of the 1830s, artistic alienation is uppermost. The broad lines of the doctrine are well known
and require only brief comment here.

Since 'le beau est supérieur à tout autre concept',[42] artistic
purity can be preserved only by ensuring that inspiration is
uncontaminated by extraneous commitments, whatever the supposed justification: 'l'art pour l'art signifie un travail dégagé de
toute préoccupation autre que celle du beau en lui-même'.[43] The
aim of poetry being categorically not the communication of ideas,
still less the proposal of any ethical or moral standpoint, it follows
that the true work of art regards subject-matter as irrelevant: 'les
sujets sont indifférents et ne valent que par l'idéal, le sentiment
et le style que chaque artiste y apporte'.[44] The ultimate absurdity
for Gautier is the notion of the direct social accountability of the
artist, the idea that he must contribute to the material progress of
his times in some approved manner. Quite apart from the mean-
inglessness of the concept of progress ('Que c'est une sotte chose
que cette prétendue perfectibilité du genre humain!' he mocks in
the 'Préface' to *Mademoiselle de Maupin*), the cult of beauty, he
claims in a frequently quoted passage of the same work, is
diametrically opposed to that of utility:

Il n'y a de vraiment beau que ce qui ne peut servir à rien; tout ce qui
est utile est laid; car c'est l'expression de quelque besoin; et ceux de
l'homme sont ignobles et dégoûtants, comme sa pauvre et infirme nature.

Poets may therefore pride themselves on being as superfluous as
the Biblical lily or a lofty mountain peak: 'Ils ne rapportent rien
et ne sont pas utiles' ('Dans la Sierra', *E*). The poet's only 'duty'
is to express his vision of the ideal:

> Rêveur harmonieux, tu fais bien de chanter:
> C'est là le seul devoir que Dieu donne aux poètes,
> Et le monde à genoux les devrait écouter.
> ('Le Triomphe de Pétrarque', *CM*).

In practice, however, Gautier's doctrine is not as extreme as
this would appear; his position on the question of the 'usefulness'
of art is more flexible than is sometimes supposed. As early as
1836 he rejected art's ingrowing tendency, and he returns to the
point later:

Est-ce à dire . . . que l'art doive se renfermer dans un indifférentisme de parti-pris, dans un détachement glacial de toute chose vivace et contemporaine pour n'admirer, Narcisse idéal, que sa propre réflexion dans l'eau et devenir amoureux de lui-même? Non . . .![45]

Gautier would in fact agree with Baudelaire that an extreme aestheticism, excluding the spiritual, was a recipe for sterility, and he accordingly came to accept 'applied' art as a means of adding a spiritual dimension to daily reality[46] and even to preach a union between art and industry.[47]

In spite of the tradition which persists in considering Gautier as a purely external artist therefore, he did in fact constantly stress that art must seek 'quelque chose au-delà de ce qui est',[48] since 'le désir le plus profond de l'âme est de sortir de l'enveloppe qui la tient prisonnière'.[49] Basically, he accepts the romantic notion of the civilising mission of the artist:

> Sur l'autel idéal entretenez la flamme,
> Guidez le peuple au bien par le chemin du beau.
> ('Le Triomphe de Pétrarque', *CM*).

ART AND THE ARTIFICIAL

Art is, then, essentially divine in nature and inspiration, and with a godlike jealousy of its independence and uniqueness. But what are the immediate practical concerns of the artist as man, directing and elaborating his creation? What recognisable character will the true work of art assume to the public? Here Gautier is consistent and uncompromising: the artistic spirit and purpose may be ultimately divine; but art itself is a human activity and its end product is clearly man-made. Art is, by definition, non-natural, 'artificial'.[50] The key principle established by Gautier and which remains his criterion for any work is that of the patent inferiority of nature to art. If the essence of reality is spiritual, it follows that external nature has no intrinsic value and constantly disappoints by its imperfection. In a celebrated anecdote Gautier recalls his adolescent disappointment at his first sight of a studio nude, 'tant l'art ajoute à la nature la plus parfaite' (*SR* 6), and later, in his travels, he frequently notes nature's mediocrity. Nature is, in fact, in spite of occasional exceptional achievements which provoke the poet's enthusiasm, gross, inert, an indiscriminate chaos of unfulfilled potentiality. Gautier would have endorsed Wilde's witticism (indebted to Gautier), that nature has good intentions but fails to carry them out,[51] proclaiming himself: 'la nature est stupide, sans conscience d'elle-même, sans pensée ni passion . . . l'art est plus beau, plus vrai, plus puissant que la nature'.[52] Gautier's ultimate paradox, 'la nature est une invention de peintres',[53] conceals a profound truth—the capacity of art to condition our way of looking at reality.

Clearly the first duty of the artist is to underline the incompatibility of nature and art by rejecting the mimetic principle: 'le but de l'art . . . n'est pas la reproduction exacte de la nature' (*HR* 216). The task is rather to conceal the inadequacy of nature and turn its poverty into richness; art is 'le vêtement que Dieu a filé de ses mains pour habiller la nudité du monde'.[54] Consequently, Gautier condemns anything which savours of unadorned realism or 'truth to life'. He castigates 'le besoin du vrai, si repoussant qu'il soit' as characteristic of an inferior art, 'dénué complètement d'esthétique' (*VE* 50). Wherever the unique quality of the Vénus de Milo resides, it is not related to any notion of 'realism',[55] for indeed 'l'illusion est une chose peu importante dans l'art; jamais un tableau de Michel-Ange ou de Raphaël n'a trompé l'œil une minute'.[56] Gautier's favourite artists exemplify such principles; for example, Watteau's escapism is allied to his 'charmante fausseté'[57]: 'Son œuvre charmant est comme un Elysée où l'esprit se console des brutalités du réalisme'.[58] For Gautier as for Baudelaire, primitive man's urge to paint his body is itself proof of an innate idealism,[59] of his refusal to be relegated to a mere mechanism satisfied with his natural needs. Hence too, above all, Gautier's admiration for the decorative arts, for 'il faut mettre au premier rang les décorateurs'.[60] Gautier's dramatic criticism is likewise based on these principles.[61]

Art, then, far from being identifiable with observable reality, is radically different from and superior to it; it produces 'une création dans une création'.[62] For the artist, strictly unable to invent forms outside nature, owing to the limitations of the human imagination, decomposes and then rearranges nature, accomplishing a transformation of reality:

Si le type de la beauté existe dans son esprit à l'état idéal, [l'artiste] prend à la nature des signes dont il a besoin pour les exprimer. Ces signes, il les transforme; il y ajoute et en ôte ... de telle sorte qu'un objet qui, dans la réalité, n'exciterait aucune attention, prend de l'importance et du charme étant représenté; car les sacrifices et les mensonges du peintre lui ont donné du sentiment, de la passion, du style et de la beauté.[63]

In this sense the artist creates unique artefacts, in divine fashion. Gautier's definition of the Petit Cénacle ideal expresses his own ambitious programme: 'sanctifier et déifier l'Art regardé comme second créateur' (*HR* 64). The capacity of art to transform reality is again uppermost in Gautier's thoughts in his 1868 essay on Baudelaire, where he enthuses over Baudelaire's stipulation that 'avant d'entrer dans la sphère de l'art, tout objet subît une métamorphose' (*SR* 291); and noteworthy in this connection is the artist's ability to incorporate potentially disruptive or alien material into his creation: the trivial, the homely,[64] the ugly even,[65] on condition that all submit to the creative imagination. This attitude was noted approvingly by Baudelaire in 1861 in his analysis of Gautier: 'il n'a aimé que le Beau; il n'a cherché que le Beau: et quand un objet grotesque ou hideux s'est offert à ses yeux, il a su encore en extraire une mystérieuse et symbolique beauté!'[66]

Clearly therefore, beauty for Gautier is certainly not limited—whatever the traditional view of him—to conventional prettiness or to the classical ideal. His work displays a lifelong addiction to the hybrid and bizarre, besides generally glorifying the 'grotesque' principle of irregularity and eccentricity[67] and frequently disparaging classical solemnity and rigidity. His admiration constantly goes to artists who have exploited a baroque imagination in the deployment of contorted or somehow unnerving forms, such as is found in gothic art, in Michelangelo or Delacroix, and, in literature, in his beloved 'Grotesques', or in Baudelaire's 'goût excessif, baroque, antinaturel' (*SR* 296). A sense of disquiet or apprehension, a 'saisissement et une admiration qui n'est pas sans quelque terreur' (*MM* 153) is often Gautier's reaction when confronted with a work of supreme genius. He who looks on beauty is awestruck, doomed. The Gautier who belittled journalism for its dependence on fact, who

.   .

objected to being treated as a mere 'larbin descriptif'[68] and who viewed with dismay the advent of the Realist school is quite clear that art should have no truck with the predictable, the unadventurous or the photographic.[69]

Far from adopting a 'naturalistic' approach to artistic creation therefore, Gautier is preoccupied with artifice. The function of the external world is strictly limited for him: it is a servicing department to the imagination, a stimulus to the real creative act, of value solely because 'il faut que l'artiste cherche son alphabet dans le monde visible, qui lui fournit ses signes conventionnels'.[70] Nature is a dictionary, to plunder and rearrange at will—a lesson taught him by his long admiration for Delacroix, and later to be re-emphasised by Baudelaire in the *Salon* of 1859 (*BOC* 1037-8, 1041). Gautier's reality has a subjective focus, for 'il faut à toute chose exprimée une incidence de lumière, un sentiment, une touche qui trahissent l'âme de l'artiste'. Otherwise, he concludes in a criticism of the realist Henri Monnier,[71] art is no longer art, 'c'est de la sténographie'. Gautier's reality is in fact rigorously organised, sifted, heightened and stylised. The implications for Gautier's poetry of these various 'artificial' processes will be considered in a later chapter.

THE DISCIPLINE OF ART

Although the poet's nature is, as we have seen, ultimately divine, Gautier anticipates Valéry by almost a century in drawing a sharp distinction between this irrational, elevated state and the actual faculties and operations needed to transform this state into meaningful activity. He is uncompromising in attacking the fallacy that inspiration is, by itself, sufficient to create a work of great art: 'L'inspiration doit trouver sous ses mains un clavier parfaitement juste, auquel ne manque aucune corde' (*HR* 336). Gautier shares Baudelaire's hostility to 'les amateurs du délire' and his repugnance for unbridled spontaneity, noting approvingly: 'les poètes *inspirés*, n'ayant pas la conscience et la direction de leur œuvre, lui causaient une sorte d'aversion'.[72] Spontaneity is not a properly poetic attribute,[73] facility must be 'purged' as a 'crime', since it entails the risk of negligence,[74] and he is critical of the use of artificial stimulants to creation because they cloud the artist's lucidity and subvert his will-power.[75] Yeats later perfectly caught Gautier's approach when he declared:

Violent energy . . . is useless in the arts. Our fire must burn slowly, and we must be content . . . to show . . . as little as the watch-mender shows, his magnifying glass caught in his screwed-up eye.[76]

Thus the poet finally—after the romantic period in which emotive value was a central issue—ceases to be the plaything of a fortuitous, wayward inspiration, to become a craftsman whose spirit works consciously and lucidly, mindful of its own integrity and discipline. The true artist for Gautier is thus a Maker, a 'faiseur' in his own expression: 'Le mot poète veut dire littéralement *faiseur*: tout ce qui n'est pas bien *fait* n'existe pas'.[77] The same strict sense applies to his declaration: 'J'ai fait *Emaux et Camées*' ('Préface', *EC*).

The stress on art as a making means that the capacity to create worthwhile artefacts depends primarily, once the initial gift is allowed, on purely volitional attributes, and this enables Gautier to speak of 'determining' the work of art. He praises, again in the essay on Baudelaire, his subject's 'mathématique infaillible', his 'délibération' and 'volonté', Baudelaire's stress on the 'voulu' as opposed to the 'accidentel', and the qualities praised repeatedly by Gautier in his criticism—concentration, effort, self-discipline invention, precision, attention to detail, *facture*—reveal the same emphasis. 'L'art, c'est la beauté, l'invention perpétuelle du détail, le choix de mots, le soin exquis de l'exécution', he proclaimed.[78]

The immediate practical result of obedience to such directives is to produce a predominantly concrete art, opposed to the fluid or 'flottant'. Gautier demands of art a certain plastic quality, confessing himself to be 'plus plastique que littéraire'.[79] It is characteristic of him that, visiting opera or ballet, he should pay less attention to the music than to *décor*, costume and movement; he admits himself to being 'moins épris de beaux sons que de beaux contours' ('La Diva', *CM*). As a guiding principle, therefore, his doctrine rejects the musical element in poetry as associated with formlessness, advising 'fuyez toujours l'épithète musicale pour l'épithète qui peint'.[80]

A short step separates the plastic from the sculptural, and Gautier constantly assimilates the poet to the sculptor, for 'le marbre et le vers sont deux matières également dures à travailler, mais les seules qui gardent éternellement la forme qu'on leur confiie'.[81] 'Mettez l'idée au fond de la forme sculptée', he counsels ('Le Triomphe de Pétrarque', *CM*). The reason for the selection of the sculptor, rather than the musician or even the painter, as king among artists, is significant. Unlike other artists, the sculptor is unable to create in a fever of inspiration, since his materials impose a physical obstacle to such a process; he of all artists must master and manipulate his medium perfectly and painstakingly, struggling with intractable matter to encapsulate his vision. The poet's task too is 'sculpter la beauté' (*HR* 359). All art, indeed, results from a struggle of the will over refractory nature, 'le moyen de surmonter les obstacles que la nature oppose à la cristallisation de la pensée'.[82] and Gautier speaks of the artist's gift as 'un marteau qui *repousse* les formes à la manière des orfèvres, et leur donne les creux et les saillies de ses préoccupations'.[83] Only in this way, as the poem-manifesto 'L'Art' proclaims, can the artist ensure that durability which is the supreme triumph of art over transient nature, stamping permanence on impermanence.[84]

Gautier is accordingly led to revive the common Renaissance and eighteenth-century notion of the 'difficulté vaincue',[85] and to stress the artist's need to commit himself to intractable formal structures: 'Je suis convaincu qu'une mesure donnée, loin de nuire à un artiste de génie, l'aide, le soutient, et lui fait trouver des ressources à quoi il n'aurait pas songé' (*VE* 127). In spite of his injunction in 'L'Art' 'point de contraintes fausses', therefore, he is not averse to the setting-up of arbitrary technical obstacles in order to sharpen and stimulate the artist's faculties; and indeed, 'le poète se plaît à cette lutte' (*HR* 312). The more rebellious the medium the greater will be the virtuosity of the triumph of this 'perpétuelle tension de l'esprit, l'effort sans repos, la lutte avec la difficulté créée à plaisir, la fatigue de rouler ce bloc de la phrase, plus pesant que celui de Sisyphe'.[86] Consequently Gautier readily commits himself to structures like the unprepossessing octosyllabic quatrain, the difficult *terza rima* and sonnet, to provocatively irregular metrical patterns when occasion warrants, and to equally challenging diversions like the *monorime* or *bouts-rimés* of which he became, as Bergerat reminds us (*EB* 98–9), an accredited master. Two significant illustrations are the prestige he attributes to rhyme and his veneration for the sonnet.

Gautier considered rhyme an essential, integral element of the poetic craft to which any aspiring poet must devote serious study (cf. *EB* 122): 'tout est bien pourvu qu'on ait la rime' ('A un Jeune Tribun', *CM*). Rhyme is a compositional priority, and examination of successive variants in a poem reveals how individual rhymes can dominate his imagination to the extent of determining the development of stanza and even poem[87]—a striking illustration of his dictum 'de la forme naît l'idée'.[88]

If skill in rhyming is one proof of 'difficulté vaincue', mastery of the difficult sonnet form is prized by Gautier as the ultimate poetic achievement. The sonnet is reverently described as 'cette forme si artistement construite, d'un rythme si justement balancé et d'une pureté qui n'admet aucune tache' (*HR* 308), and again as 'cette forme charmante, taillée à facettes comme un flacon de cristal, et si merveilleusement propre à contenir une goutte de lumière ou d'essence'.[89] For the Gautier who fulminates against verbosity, the virtue of the sonnet is precisely in its economy, its severity, its capacity to mould thought inside the strait-jacket of a fixed form: 'l'idée entrant dans le sonnet qui la contient, l'amincit et en assure le contour' (*HR* 345). The true artist alone

> ... possède au plus haut degré la concision, la texture serrée du style et du vers, l'art de réduire une image en une épithète, la hardiesse d'ellipse, l'ingéniosité subtile et l'adresse d'emménager dans la place circonscrite ... une foule d'idées, de mots et de détails qui demanderaient ailleurs des pages entières aux vastes périodes (*HR* 346).

Elsewhere Gautier defines the sonnet as 'une sorte de fugue poétique', an art of counterpoint based on resolution of artistic tensions through 'les formes voulues'.[90] One of the enduring glories of the romantic school, he points out (*HR* 344), was, following the lead given by Sainte-Beuve, to have rehabilitated the sonnet of Petrarch and Ronsard, and he is proud of his own contribution to this poetic renewal.[91] Although usually associated with the octosyllabic quatrain, owing to the celebrity of *Emaux et Camées*, Gautier did, in fact, compose more sonnets than poems in any other single form, and it must therefore be considered his favourite poetic structure.[92]

Naturally, the overall emphasis on the formal disciplines of art largely excludes the lyrical as 'bourgeois', facile and vulgar: 'Demander à la poésie du sentimentalisme . . . ce n'est pas ça!'[93] The rôle of the artist is not to evoke sympathy, but rather to indulge himself in a solo display of virtuoso craftsmanship without compromising his essential emotional neutrality. Gautier accepts the lyrical only on condition that it be severely disciplined; and indeed the apparently unbridled lyricism of the romantics hid, in effect, he observes in an essay on Berlioz, 'une science technique profonde': 'Tous ces prétendus artistes échevelés, sans frein, qui, soi-disant, n'écrivaient que sous l'inspiration de la fièvre chaude, étaient au contraire des *contrapuntistes* consommés' (*HR* 263). Emotion must be treated intellectually, and art becomes the rational sublimation of a sensual impetus, represented best by the kind of aerial lyricism Gautier praised in Banville (*HR* 300–5). Such art clearly places a premium on Parnassian impersonality, and the term 'dehumanisation' has been applied to Gautier with some justice.[94] Gautier had great admiration for Leconte de Lisle's haughty elitism (cf. *HR* 330, 334), declaring himself: 'Rien n'est plus insupportable que le "moi" . . . Nous nous réduisons autant que possible à n'être qu'un œil détaché'.[95] Gautier loved to visualise himself in later life serenely withdrawn from life's bustle, like the allegedly impassive 'Goethe, l'olympien'.[96]

The corollary to the view of poetry as a pure formal diversion is seen in its extreme form in the notion of it as a mere arrangement of words to which overall subject is quite subservient. The absorption of the poet-aesthete in formal problems of language is very clearly seen in Gautier, who stresses the intrinsic value of words as entities with a creativity of their own: 'Pour le poète, les mots ont, en eux-mêmes et en dehors du sens qu'ils expriment, une beauté et une valeur propres'.[97] Or again, he declares: 'Les mots des poètes conservent du sens même quand ils sont détachés des autres, et plaisent isolés comme de beaux sons' (*HR* 301–2). Words possess an almost magic power, reminding us that it was Gautier to whom Baudelaire applied his celebrated phrase 'sorcellerie évocatoire' (*BOC* 690).

Gautier took an intense delight in words intrinsically. His

'lexicomania' was legendary enough to warrant his inclusion in Balzac's celebrated boast: 'Nous sommes trois à Paris qui savons notre langue, Hugo, Gautier et moi'.[98] Baudelaire comments on Gautier's immense vocabulary, 'ce magnifique dictionnaire' (*BOC* 689), while Bergerat recalls the poet's pride in his contribution to the French language and his confidence that posterity would not refuse him 'ce modeste mérite de philologue' (*EB* 115). Gautier went so far as to proclaim: 'Celui qu'une pensée, fût-ce la plus complexe, une vision, fût-ce la plus apocalyptique, surprend sans mots pour les réaliser, n'est pas un écrivain' (*EB* 117). It is not surprising therefore that, whatever else it was for Gautier, poetry should be first and foremost the art of manipulating words. Content is devalued, form dominates, poetry is 'une façon de phrase, un certain choix de mots'.[99] Gautier would have approved Mallarmé's celebrated rejoinder to Degas:—'Ce n'est point avec des idées . . . que l'on fait des vers. C'est avec des *mots*'.[100]

Yet for the self-avowed 'fils du soleil'[101] who claimed 'la lumière est la forme du Verbe',[102] poetry is not indiscriminate verbosity, but rather 'des mots rayonnants, des mots de lumière . . . avec un rythme et une musique'.[103] For 'les mots vibrent et flambent, harmonies et rayons'.[104] He is even more precise: 'Il y a des mots diamants, saphir, rubis, émeraude, d'autres qui luisent comme du phosphore quand on les frotte'.[105] The artist sifts this array of words 'riches, brillants et rares' (*HR* 301–2): 'il les trie . . . comme ferait un orfèvre méditant un bijou',[106] before deploying them skilfully:

il les place sertis d'or autour de son idée comme un bracelet de pierreries autour d'un bras de femme . . . Les mots s'illuminent quand le doigt du poète fait passer son phosphore (*HR* 301–2).

Thus the craftsman merges not only with the showman, since special stress is laid on virtuosity, but with the magician.

Consequently Gautier is nostalgic for his beloved pre-classical sixteenth century with its love of exuberant stylistic mannerisms from which he plunders: 'J'ai fourragé à pleines mains dans le seizième siècle . . . je suis revenu la hotte pleine, avec des gerbes et des fusées' (*EB* 117). It is often necessary to accentuate contrasts, to spice one's style with 'un feu d'artifice de mots, des bombes lumineuses de métaphores, des pluies d'argent et d'or, d'adjectifs et de comparaisons'.[107]

Gautier's poetic doctrine then, viewed as a whole, appears as an attempt, not always consistent and often erratic, at merging traditionally opposed views of the poet's art. Ever conscious of its mysterious origins, art attempts to recapture for man his lost divinity; but this is possible only on condition that it proclaims its autonomy and cultivates, even to excess, its particular disciplines to the exclusion of all other considerations. The result is an art which is self-contained, 'qui ne tire ses formes que de lui-même' (*VI* 113). The preoccupation with form, potentially sterile as Gautier recognises, hides nevertheless a major virtue:

... car, de même qu'un motif jaillit sous les doigts du musicien laissant errer ses doigts sur les touches, une idée, une image résultent souvent des chocs de mots évoqués pour les nécessités métriques (*HR* 337).

Like Banville, Gautier stresses that the poet is an 'ouvrier', but his work is more than a craft: it can become an alchemy, capable of accomplishing not only that ambitious, peculiarly modern programme of 'la fusion des arts entre eux'[108] of which Gautier speaks with personal pride,[109] but looking forward ultimately to that concept of art as a metaphysical quest which first Nerval and Baudelaire and then the Symbolists were to develop and enrich.

III

GAUTIER'S POETRY

Gautier's concept of poetry and the very nature of his inspiration ensure that no grouping of his prolific poetic output is entirely satisfactory. Concerned with parts rather than the whole, Gautier's approach is inconsequential. Lacking *souffle*, he excels in the short poem; his inspiration is essentially occasional, fragmented; once written, the poem stands alone, an isolated unit. And Gautier was both too busy and too dilatory to attempt himself to regroup his poems in any meaningful way. It follows that each *recueil* is a largely artificial unit of convenience lacking internal structure, a disparate miscellany of short poems arbitrarily juxtaposed under a somewhat neutral, uninformative title.

Nevertheless, a certain progression is discernible in Gautier's poetic career viewed as a whole; and whatever the obvious shortcomings of the commonly accepted view of two clear-cut phases (a 'première manière' or 'manière romantique' preceding an impassive maturity), a twofold division with the break around 1840 would appear the most practicable approach to the question of his poetic development. Gautier himself lent support to such a chronological division by claiming, in an oft-quoted letter to Sainte-Beuve,[1] that around 1838 he consciously renounced subjective inspiration in favour of a more objective manner (though this is clearly an oversimplification). Significantly, it has been noted[2] that 1838 also marks the approximate date from which Gautier's use of the octosyllable and the sonnet, suggesting an increasing formal preoccupation, began noticeably to predominate, and the end of a vigorous, independent approach in his art criticism.[3] So far as the argument about a writer's evolution is at all meaningful, therefore, evidence does seem to indicate a turning-point, even perhaps a decision taken, soon after the appearance of *La Comédie de la Mort*.

It is surely true that, viewed together, those volumes published or composed prior to 1840 present what Bergerat terms a 'militantisme romantique' (*EB* 51). *Poésies*, *Albertus* and *La Comédie de la Mort*, particularly when read in conjunction with contemporary prose works like *Les Jeunes-France*, *Les Grotesques*, *Mademoiselle de Maupin* and 'Fortunio', represent 'semi-fashionable' genres, subscribing (though not always with total seriousness) to a variety of stock romantic postures: sentimental and naïve in *Poésies*, truculently Byronic in *Albertus*, luridly tortured in *La Comédie de la Mort*. These volumes are all basically inward-looking, introspective, romantic in the sense of depending for effect on intensely emotional responses to life.

The poetry composed after 1840, on the other hand, appears in general, after the transitional *España*, as a progressive departure from the romantic Grand Manner—even though one can now see clearly that *La Comédie de la Mort* is categorically not, as Maxime du Camp claimed (op. cit., p. 168), 'l'adieu de Gautier au romantisme'. Literary expediency no doubt played its part in this evolution: aware of the exhaustion of certain stock areas of romanticism, Gautier, perhaps consciously, wishes to find new types of expression. No doubt losing confidence in his ability to sustain a lofty theme, the poet appears increasingly aware of his true nature as he turns from the familiar, often borrowed emotionalism to saner, less rhetorical territory and begins to explore a more restricted genre. As one recent commentator has put it,[4] Gautier appears as a romantic 'lowering his sights', 'narrowing his scope', expurgating the theatrical and flamboyant, sifting and translating experience into an authentically original manner.

For convenience, the following sections on Gautier's poetry treat of the successive *recueils* in chronological progression. It must not be forgotten, however, that this order does not necessarily correspond to that in which individual poems were composed.

THE EARLY POETRY, 1830–40

Poésies (1830, 1832)

Gautier's first volume was published on 28 July 1830 and comprised forty-two short poems. As its publication coincided with the July Revolution virtually no copies were sold and, 'sombré dans la tempête' (*SR* 9), it was consequently withdrawn. It was then enlarged by the addition of twenty new poems, enlivened by the flamboyant 'Albertus' and a provocative 'Préface', and republished in October 1832 under the general title *Albertus*. For the 1830 volume of *Poésies*, the critical edition by H. Cockerham (Athlone Press, 1973) should be consulted. The present section discusses the enlarged, 1832 edition as a whole, but excluding the poem 'Albertus'.

The traditional view of *Poésies* has been insistently dismissive. Heavy stress has been laid on the derivative nature of the poetic material and critics have been mainly concerned to establish the many direct borrowings from numerous romantic sources. It is of course undeniable that the reader progressing through this collection is constantly struck by echoes of, or even actual phrases from Goethe, Byron, Chateaubriand, Lamartine, Sainte-Beuve, Hugo, Musset and others, and these borrowings have been faithfully recorded by René Jasinski in *Les Années Romantiques* and in his edition of the *Poésies Complètes*.

It seems doubtful, however, whether the critical attention devoted to this question of 'sources' is fully justified by the results, which have tended to prove simply that the borrowings are numerous and varied, and to suggest—predictably—an adolescent strongly marked by fashionable contemporary writers. Quite apart from the fact that Gautier himself made little secret of the derivative nature of much of his material[5] and in any case disparaged the conventional view of what constitutes originality,[6] it is surely more profitable to enquire what elements of individuality rather than of conformity are present. Examination of the volume as a whole suggests, in fact, that a marked individuality is already emerging and that the collection's most characteristic poems belong to neither the intimate domestic genre of Sainte-Beuve (cf. 'Le Coin du Feu', 'Veillée'), nor the Hugolian 'epistle' (cf. 'A mon ami Eugène de N***', 'Soleil Couchant'), even less the gothic (cf. 'Moyen Age', 'Cauchemar'); but rather to a muted vein Gautier was to make peculiarly his own.

The 'Préface' of 1832 itself clearly indicates the general character of the volume by proclaiming certain tenets that Gautier will never subsequently renounce: the integrity of the artist in an age of insidious philistinism, the notion of the sublime superfluity of art, and the rejection of literary ostentation. The latter point is especially noteworthy, since in rejecting pretentiousness ('ni grandes montagnes, ni perspectives à perte de vue, ni torrents,

ni cataractes') the young Gautier is clearly sceptical of romanticism's prevailing *fortissimo* moods. A little later, indeed, Gautier
associated a 'poète malsain' specifically with his 'vertige du
grandiose'.[7] For Gautier, 'me faisant du bonheur avec la moindre
chose' ('Enfantillage'), the narrowness, the banalities of adolescent experience are to be artistically sufficient; and in thus
making a virtue of necessity, he is already withdrawing towards
the voluntary constriction which will become a hallmark of his
poetic individuality—even though he is unable to resist, with the
flamboyant 'Albertus', adventuring for a moment into the already
well-worn territory of romantic sensationalism.

If the inclusion of certain titles ('Enfantillage', 'La Jeune
Fille', 'Les Souhaits') were not sufficient in itself to define the
individuality of *Poésies*, the pink cover chosen for the first edition
appropriately symbolised the prevailing note of contrived naïvety
of this 'poésie tout enfantine, toute ronde et potelée' ('Préface'),
this 'enfant à la grâce ingénue, avec son collier fait de perles de
rosée' ('Pensée de Minuit', *CM*). It is this type of *préciosité*, rather
than the quantitatively unimportant gothic element which has
been curiously overstressed,[8] which appears the true character of
the volume; and to this we shall return.

There is nevertheless a greater variety of inspiration in *Poésies*
than is usually allowed. Apart from the conscious imitations of
earlier models in the enumeration of stock romantic preoccupations (in 'Elégie I' a potential mistress is a devotee of Richardson
and Goethe's *Werther*), there are many direct autobiographical
stimulants: a variety of shadowy but perhaps sincere affairs
('Elégie II', 'Déclaration', 'Nonchaloir', 'Le Bengali'); parodies
of Jeunes-France extravagance from first-hand experience
('Cauchemar', 'Débauche'); friendship and love of art ('A mon
ami Eugène de N***'); family visits to Mauperthuis ('Voyage',
'Le Sentier'); and the exhilaration of Paris in its various aspects—
sylvan ('Le Luxembourg', 'Le Jardin des Plantes'), aesthetic
('Soleil Couchant') or realistic ('Pan de Mur', 'Paris'). In addition, there are hints of the poet's growing disillusion with
contemporary life ('Sonnet VII': 'Avec ce siècle infâme . . .'),
inspiring tantalising snatches of Gautier's talent for social satire.

Yet it is usually in the absence of any direct external stimulant
such as these that the most characteristic note is heard. Having

lived a relatively sheltered family existence, 'éloigné des choses de la vie', the poet confesses his ignorance of life by his dependence on the trivia of a leisured, dilettante existence of idle day-dreaming: 'Qu'il fait bon ne rien faire . . .!' ('Ballade'). For the young Gautier the poet's first attribute is a watchful indolence, a deceptive inactivity, whether reclining in a boudoir ('Nonchaloir'), basking doodling in the sunshine ('Far Niente', 'Le Retour'), sauntering in the park ('Le Jardin des Plantes', 'Le Luxembourg') or dreaming by the fireside ('Veillée', 'Le Coin du Feu'). A constant preoccupation with self is apparent: 'J'aime à m'écouter vivre' ('Far Niente'), 'm'oublier moi-même' ('Nonchaloir'), together with nostalgia for the past ('Ballade', 'Le Retour', 'Imitation de Byron'). Much of the volume constitutes a 'rose et suave peinture où soi-même l'on pose' ('Le Retour'). Narcissism is checked, however, by the poet's fascination with the two major themes of *Poésies*, nature and love, both treated largely through their external manifestations. The focus is predominantly formal, plastic rather than emotional, as brief examination of each in turn will illustrate.

The large incidence of rural inspiration in *Poésies* may seem strange, in view of the frequent disparagement of the countryside by this 'Parisien complet' ('Préface', *Les Jeunes-France*). Yet the paradox is more apparent than real. For the city adolescent, the sheer novelty of the annual holiday at Mauperthuis was irresistible: the enforced idleness of exile, with a suggestion of first love in idyllic surroundings, provided a sedentary youth with a congenial artistic diversion—that of exploiting the natural environment as a spur to fanciful creation. Gautier's method is far from objective: a poem like 'Paysage' is exceptional. External reality 'exists', but because its constituents are of unequal artistic value a rigorous selection takes place in favour of privileged items of a rare or delicate character in form, colour, contour; birds, flowers, insects even. The poet-painter concentrates on the diminutive to the exclusion of wider horizons: the frail anemone, the sheen of a duck's plumage, the glint of a lizard's eye, gossamer and dewdrops, a bee entering a flower, and this world glistens and shimmers with a springtime freshness. In fact, within the already restricted genre of the traditional 'nature poem' a further process of elimination is taking place, determining a transformation of reality by a complex of techniques: formalisation, stylisation, pictorialism. Each of these processes requires brief comment.

Averse to the *fortissimo* as we have noted, the poet aims to create 'de petits paysages . . . d'une touche tranquille' ('Préface'). Such a process entails the translation of violence or adversity into either conventional posturings in which plastic, almost allegorical, representation replaces realism (an arched eyebrow and curled lip hold a world of grief: 'Sonnet vi'), or else its emasculation in inanimate, stylised form. Disaster may be reduced to meteorological form, acquiring either the picturesqueness of abstract pattern (rain is 'des filets gris rayant un ciel noir' in 'L'Oiseau Captif'), or suggesting inappropriate decorative metaphors (a rain-cloud is 'un beau cheval arabe' in 'Pluie'). Storms are splendidly theatrical, calling for contorted trees, windows beseiged by demoniacal forces and, in this fanciful Ile-de-France, avalanches crumbling into the abyss! The undercurrent of latent violence, the presence of evil in nature is thus checked or attenuated by the deployment of plastic imagery over which the poet retains control. Nature is exploited contrapuntally, these catastrophes being orchestrated to enhance the recurrent dream-world, a comforting oasis of sunlight, warmth and serenity:

> Je veux un beau soleil qui luise dans l'azur,
> Sans que jamais brouillard, vapeur, nuage obscur
> Ne voilent son orbe splendide.
>
> ('Les Souhaits')

The process of assimilating human anguish to equivalences in nature easily results in the substitution of prettiness for profundity. In 'Méditation' human decadence is seen as part of a wider natural process, but the theme is charmingly illustrated rather than analysed; in 'Sonnet i' faith has ebbed yet the poet is content to note visual and auditive sensation; in 'Les Deux Ages' maturity menaces the adolescent, but the emphasis is on past rather than present. Constantly important human issues are broached only to be skirted round and lost in a welter of plastic imagery.

The stylisation of nature is particularly evident in the choice of vocabulary. Not only does neo-classic diction abound ('brise', 'onde', 'azur', 'grève', 'flots') but this is allied to a process of idealisation. 'Gazon' and 'pré', often further prettified to 'émail velouté' or 'velours vert', are substituted for the pedestrian 'herbe' or 'champ'. The sky is 'azur' or 'pourpre'; 'blés' are not only golden but, formalised, 'égaux', while dew, tears, and pearls are infinitely interchangeable. Lakes are glassily 'limpides', and their 'eau d'argent', fringed with 'sable d'or', contains aquarium fish.

A further urge towards over-organisation of reality is reflected in the geometricalisation of natural motifs: *Poésies* contains not only architectural contours but also many arching fountains, chequered 'champs bariolés', circling insects, rippling water, looping streams and other sinuous forms. Nature is usually either crystallised into glittering jewel-like effects, like the favourite image of the butterfly, 'écrin ailé', or textured like some rich tapestry of almost abstract patterns. In the few urban landscapes too, a similar formalisation is evident, as in 'Pan de Mur', where the plane of the wall is broken successively by obliques, zigzags, squares and spirals. Serrated roofs, spiky towers and swirling smoke disturb skylines. Distant town prospects become grotesquely animated: chimneys like ships' masts tear apart livid clouds snaking across murky horizons in 'Frisson' (cf. 'Point de Vue').

Very characteristic of *Poésies* is the creation, through careful choice of vocabulary and motifs, of a delicately refined vision. The poet stresses the fastidious, the dainty and the fragile not only visually, in the microscopic detail of fauna and flora, but in the other sense-registers too. Thus the overall tonality becomes delicately ephemeral, almost insubstantial, in a world in which nothing mundane, no element of the *grisâtre*, must intrude. Nor is all the imagery conventionally pretty: knotted trunks, weeds growing in a fissured, rain-washed wall, the trail of a slug are all incorporated into the poetic vision, dissociated from familar experience. Some notations are exquisitely observed: the 'moites réseaux' of the rivulet, the swan's reflection on the water, fringed eyelashes, vaulting stained with sunlight filtered through glass, a coal fire's transmutations, the pirouetting weather vane,

> La lumière brisant dans chacun de mes cils,
> Palissade opposée à ses rayons subtils.
>> ('Far Niente')

Within this rarefied world is revealed an intense but microscopic activity, coupled with much fanciful myth-making. In this realm of Titania or Ariel many a hushed Lilliputian drama is being enacted, and this miniaturism is a further process of distancing from reality. Bees plunder, ants steal, beetles drowse, ducks frolic, dragonflies fuss, insects drown. This discreet anthropomorphism with its potentially satiric element is motiveless however; it is playful mock-heroism, 'the triumph of insignificance',[9] a whimsical diversion, as the 'Préface' hinted.

A static or cinematographic effect is often conveyed by Gautier through his painter's habit of eyeing landscape in terms of organised planes of observation: 'ici ... là', 'à gauche ... à droite', 'plus loin', 'au premier plan', 'd'un côté ... de l'autre', 'au milieu'. Studio terminology creeps in: 'pans', 'teinte', 'palette', 'touche', 'ambre', 'tons', 'perspective'; in fact, 'c'est un tableau tout fait qui vaut qu'on l'étudie' ('Pan de Mur'). Nature, it is clearly hinted, is a supremely contrived work of art:

> Un vrai panorama vivant et bigarré,
> Par un pinceau divin ardemment coloré.
>
> ('Le Retour')

Although reality is present in this collection, therefore, it is transformed, by a series of aesthetically motivated processes, into a set of decorative tableaux composed of recurrent motifs. With precise observation as basis the poet interposes a highly imaginative personal vision, creating from the 'real' Mauperthuis or Parisian garden a self-contained artistic entity animated by a whimsical life of its own. The resultant 'poésie tout enfantine' ('Préface') has something of the naivety of the child's picture-book or the *décor* of a puppet theatre which the adult nostalgically recreates.

The poet's treatment of love follows a similar pattern. Once again realism is virtually banished. True, the loved one may be seventeen, called Maria, even have a Spanish accent, but such details are exceptional, minor concessions in a web of *préciosité* from which, in spite of banal laments in neo-classic vein and the moody protestations of 'Débauche', strong emotional involvement is patently lacking. Significantly Rioult's pupil rejects his master's erotic grand manner in favour of a more subtle, Boucher-like Arcadia:

> Je préfère pourtant ses petites baigneuses,
> Vrai chef-d'œuvre de grâce et de naiveté . . .
>   ('A mon ami Eugène de N***')

or the Watteauesque scenes of 'Frisson'. Where passion is present
ıt is used either contrapuntally as an artistic device, transferred
into conventional figures like oxymoron and hyperbole, stylised
in external plastic representation (grief almost automatically
becomes tears of pearl), or else filtered through a neo-classic
diction which robs it of immediacy of impact. Thus 'ce feu qui
dévore et qui ne s'éteint pas' is balanced by 'ses propos naïfs et
sa grâce enfantine' ('Elégie ıı'); and the style may become almost
Racinian in its studied attenuation of passion:

> Cette vague langueur et ce doux mal d'aimer,
> Pour un objet chéri ces mortelles alarmes . . .
>   ('Stances')

The use of hyperbole in particular follows the courtly love
tradition; it is no coincidence that Gautier pays tribute to the
trouvères (cf. 'A mon ami Eugène de N***') and frequently selects
epigraphs from Théophile, Marot, Baïf, Desportes and *Le Roman
de la Rose*. All the ingredients of the chivalric genre are present:
the deification of the loved one, the exaggerated solemnity, the
over-dramatisation, the mannered poses, the polarisation of concepts, the general superlativism. Love becomes an elegant pos-
turing or a languid enthralment.

The maidenly ideal celebrated is not only Petrarch's *belle*, however. Certain private attributes peculiar to Gautier's 'enfant
blanche et blonde' ('Les Deux Ages') are stressed: her extreme
youth, an arch naivety, a capricious frivolity; and every physical
attribute—swan's neck, curved eyebrows, long eyelashes, velvet
eyes, undulating hair—underpins this elusive sinuosity. The *décor*
in which this heroine is set is one of exquisite delicacy, to which
her dress of linen, satin or silk contributes. The overall effect
strikingly recalls the idealised, winsome grace of the Botticelli
Venus which later haunted Gautier's imagination and who
already seems present, fragmented, in the composite heroine of
Poésies.[10] For Gautier, as for mediaeval scholars, the story of the
birth of Venus was a symbolic representation of the divine message
of beauty to man: his own heroine is 'un souvenir des cieux' ('La

Jeune Fille'), 'ange exilé des cieux' ('Elégie III'). Gautier's ideal is in consequence largely dehumanised; his heroine is a mosaic of motifs which never comes alive psychologically, the decorative materialisation of a vision.

Finally in *Poésies*, in addition to the constant disproportion between form and content (cf. 'Maria'), certain specific features suggest the conscious stylist already at work. Unable to rival the virtuosity of Hugo's *Les Orientales* which he so profoundly admired, Gautier nevertheless skilfully exploits metrical effects in pieces like 'La Demoiselle', 'Clémence', 'Frisson', and the two 'Ballades'. In 'La Demoiselle' particularly, content and form merge perfectly to produce an exquisite, integrated whole, one of Gautier's finest early compositions. Moreover, the supposedly unmusical Gautier not only delights in the diversion of imitative verbal harmony ('des fleurs qu'un pied inattentif froisse', 'la grêle . . . fouette la vitre frêle') and gratuitous sound-patterns ('une joue ingénue', 'la rosée arrondie', 'murs moussus et noircis') but frequently achieves harmonic effects of real beauty.

The double volume of *Poésies* offers, therefore, a greater richness and interest than has often been conceded, and repays careful attention. Biographically it records not only an intellectual exhilaration but poignantly, the sense of youthful dispossession hinted at in the epigraph of the 1830 title page: 'Oh! si je puis un jour'; of being thrust into an alien world in which art is the sole refuge from the 'vilain crabe' *ennui* ('Le Cavalier Poursuivi'). Artistically it looks forward to Gautier's maturity rather than backwards to outdated models, for far from being slavishly imitative Gautier is already fascinated by the concept of art as play and preoccupied with a highly fanciful and stylised treatment of material. While reality is not absent, there is little 'realism' in the volume, external reality being usually the mere prop of a dilettante artist intent on the deployment of seemingly gratuitous forms which in fact express a private vision: for

Le but de l'art . . . n'est pas la reproduction exacte de la nature mais la création, au moyen des formes et des couleurs qu'elle nous livre, d'un microcosme où puissent habiter et se produire les rêves, les sensations et les idées que nous inspire l'aspect du monde (*HR* 216).

In this withdrawal the attempt to refine experience is associated with the plastic and verbal freedom which Gautier, following Hugo in his Preface to *Les Orientales*, terms 'caprice'. Nature and love in particular are drawn into delicate patterns of sensual motifs and transformed by what Sainte-Beuve perceptively defined as Gautier's

... habitude de tout voir à travers un certain cristal et dans un certain miroir ... une sorte de glace magique où tout se réfléchisse, se transforme et ressorte ensuite ... avec une harmonie nouvelle.[11]

This balance between intellectual delight, naivety and a delicate sensuality is already the keynote of his earliest volume, and this interplay will remain a dominant characteristic of Gautier's poetry to the end.

'Albertus' (1832)

The long narrative poem 'Albertus' was the climax of the new, enlarged edition of the unsold *Poésies* of 1830, republished in October 1832. The poem continues the exploitation, though in very different vein from that of *Poésies*, of certain fashionable aspects of romanticism, and is the first serious indication of Gautier's lifelong addiction to gothic extravaganza, of which *Poésies* had already given hints.[12] Gautier himself characterised his poem cavalierly as 'semi-diabolique, semi-fashionable' ('Préface'), suggesting a tongue-in-cheek exercise in satanic dandyism. Its inclusion in a non-existent 'cycle carlovingien' (coupled with 'La Comédie de la Mort'),[13] testified to its affectations of grandiloquence—which, however, it is clear the author did not intend entirely seriously.

'Albertus' has clearly a dual motivation. On the one hand the young poet, anxious to conquer success after the disappointment of the first *Poésies*, is consciously competing with the more spectacular side of romanticism. It represents Gautier's own contribution to the strain of *bas-romantisme* whose remarkable fortunes were still far from being exhausted, and the poem is accordingly crammed with all the stock ingredients of the genre. On the other hand the sceptical and facetious Gautier is consciously poking fun at the tradition; the new poem anticipates the forthcoming *Les Jeunes-France* in constituting a kind of 'Précieuses ridicules du romantisme' (*SR* 9), in which the portentous and delirious is constantly mocked by a comic or ironic element. Understandably, the poem's mixed reception was not without a certain *succès de scandale*,[14] and for some time after the author was known in literary circles by the name of his hero, in mock respect: 'le surnom d'Albertus me resta', records Gautier (*SR* 9), 'et l'on ne m'appelait guère autrement'.

As with *Poésies*, Gautier's debt to existing models is considerable, both in the general Faustian theme of the damnation of a fatal young hero for having tried to embrace his ideal through a pact with the devil (cf. Stanzas xciii–xcv), and in the individual episodes of the poem. As Jasinski comments, ' "Albertus" est une mosaïque de thèmes, chaque thème une mosaïque d'emprunts' (*AR* 113)—a point made tartly by adverse contemporary reviews (cf. *AR* 119ff.). It would however be naive to suppose that Gautier intended these borrowings to pass undetected. Indeed, he takes pains to remind the reader of many of them in his text, and even ventures an impudent joke about plagiarists (xiv).

In defining his poem as 'semi-diaboloque, semi-fashionable', the author himself clearly indicates his two major sources from the gothic tradition. The first element is the occult, including a hotch-potch of witchcraft, alchemy, magic, the morbid and the supernatural, all recently renewed, principally by Byron, Nodier, Goethe, Hugo and Berlioz, with a more diffuse debt to certain awesome aspects of Milton and Shakespeare. To these general precursors should be added the host of Gautier's own favourites in the genre, whose names recur through all his work: Ann Radcliffe, Rembrandt, the Goya of *Los Caprichos*, Rabelais, Piranesi and Martin, Callot, Hoffmann, Scott, Balzac, the Teniers of *The Alchemist* and, of course, Nerval's translation of *Faust* from which Gautier actually quotes (cx; cf. *AR* 103).

In this genre full rein is given to any supernatural fantasy, but Satanism in particular was much in vogue in Gautier's Petit Cénacle, as well as being a distinctive feature of the times, as he himself recalls in a contemporary article:

On ne peut aujourd'hui lire un roman, écouter un drame, entendre une romance, sans avoir l'esprit frappé de mots mystiques, de noms angéliques, diaboliques, cabalistiques. C'est une vogue . . .[15]

The horrific nature of the subject was announced at the outset by a suitable frontispiece, an engraving by the fashionable artist Célestin Nanteuil which Gautier describes as 'abracadabrante',[16] 'ultra-excentrique',[17] 'rappelant les griffonnages mystérieux et les effets bizarrement fantastiques de Rembrandt',[18] and by the epigraph from *Hamlet* (with its double error curiously perpetuated to this day).[19] Internally, the poet warns the reader with mock solemnity that this 'cynical' work is not intended for young ladies (xcviii).

The second stock element basic to the poem lies in the term 'fashionable', reminding the reader that the cult of the dandy, deriving from Brummell and Byron, was at its height in the early 1830s, merging with the Jeunes-France aesthetic of ultra-refinement and their uncompromising hostility to the supposed mediocrity of the 'bourgeois' spirit. The simultaneous popularity of Shakespeare and Byron was a characteristic of the period, and the tortured, sardonic figures of Hamlet and of 'Byron et son Don Juan moqueur' ('Pensée de Minuit', *CM*) merged with those of Satan and Faust (characters all shortly to reappear in 'La Comédie de la Mort') to become a literary stock-in-trade. The dandy was essentially an aesthete who flaunted an arrogant affectation of blasé elegance in an effort to conceal an undercurrent of doom and violence. The figure of Albertus as described in Stanzas lix ff., with his extension, the Byronic limping Beelzebub (cxiv), is simply the first of a long line of semi-autobiographical dandy heroes in Gautier's work, which has indeed been described as 'peuplé de dandys'.[20]

While it may no longer be possible to see in 'Albertus' the 'merveilleux poème' extolled by both Bergerat and Banville (*EB* 46, 233), it is unjust to dismiss it. Like much of Gautier's work the poem contains inherent ambiguities; it exists on different planes, offering a multiple interest.

It offers at its simplest level that inconsequential, 'period' charm of any work of art too precisely rooted in a specific historical period and now relegated to a picturesque remoteness. As a composite documentary on the climate of the 1830s it provides a useful and enjoyable compendium of motifs and preoccupations of the romantic heyday. Its general theme of the idealist destroyed by his quest of the absolute is itself central to much romantic thought, besides containing an eternal, intrinsic fascination.

'Albertus' also offers a clear autobiographical interest, and one of some complexity. It is usually accepted that Gautier was incapable of creating character with independent psychological life, as is proved by the succession of almost identical, patently autobiographical heroes, Albertus, d'Albert, Onuphrius, Fortunio, Tiburce, Malivert . . . These projections of Gautier's inner psyche convey the profound insecurity of the author in the image of the masterful, successful dandy or, as here, in its tragic counterpart, the Byronic hero, foredoomed, unable to reconcile ideal with reality, psychologically unbalanced. As in Byron's 'Don Juan', there is constant irony and self-denigration in Albertus-Gautier:

> . . . L'ironie,
> Le sarcasme y brillait plutôt que le génie;
> Le bas semblait railler le haut (LX)[21]

and this corrosive mockery appears as part of the author's defence mechanism against disillusion. Quite apart, therefore, from the directly confessional passages of the poem where the tone becomes serious, even moving (cf. Stanzas XLVII–LIX, LXXII, XXIII), and the private soliloquising (III, XXXVIII), it is fascinating to follow the poet's attempts to resolve the conflicts in his own nature under cover of Albertus' fictional case.

'Albertus' presents, too, a particular interest for the study of Gautier's poetic evolution. The poem shows its author impatient with the neo-classical structures and myths which partly characterised *Poésies*. After the 'touche tranquille' of the latter volume, 'Albertus' unleashes, for a time, Gautier's full Rabelaisian, Falstaffian manner[22] in an exuberant poetic orgy. The stock genre of the legend (it even purports to be based on the regulation old chronicle, an amusing pretence at authentication) is a tempting and convenient device allowing the freest of treatment: richly anecdotal, it permits abundance of asides, constant interruption and a generally erratic development. The narrator becomes an impertinent guide leading a conducted tour of the author's private fantasies. Many of these are to be among Gautier's most recurrent obsessions: the macabre and all its accessories, physical transformation in an eerie Hoffmannesque world of 'contours équivoques' (XI), the world of the arts (studio, music, theatre), including specific works of art, like Teniers' *Alchemist*, Callot's *Tentation* or the folksy genre scenes of Ostade and Brouwer. There are erotic boudoir fantasies built around a composite feminine ideal; the fascination with sharply defined plastic motifs; constant hyperbole; technical vocabulary and exotic, foreign sonorities; touches of social satire; the underlying pessimism of seeing life as a lie or masquerade and the blurring of the distinction between appearance and reality in this

> Glace vue à l'envers où l'on ne connaît rien,
> Car tout est transposé. (XI)

Typical above all perhaps is a baroque imagination at work not only in the festoons of imagery of this

> ... pandémonium!—où sur la même ligne,
> Se heurtent mille objets fantasquement mêlés (IX)

but in the ambiguous juxtaposition of comedy and horror, sincerity and cynicism, beauty and the grotesque, light and shade. Supremely baroque is the way in which the whole is conceived as a virtuoso performance of *tape-à-l'œil* ingredients. These and similar themes and mannerisms of Gautier's art are assembled here fully for the first time in a riot of fantasy, to recur constantly, if usually more discreetly, in his mature work. Moreover, no subject is immune from jaundiced, ironic treatment, not even Gautier's beloved Rubens, symbolised by 'des montagnes de chair' (XXXII), not even love itself, praised one moment as sole good in life (XLIX) only to be mocked hideously in Véronique's true self. And so 'Albertus' sees the convergence of so much that is to become distinctive in Gautier's mature artistic personality.

Finally, 'Albertus' is a *tour de force* in its own right with many intrinsic merits. The technical skill is already remarkable: vying with his models the young Gautier is not noticeably inferior, and Sainte-Beuve commented how unjust it was that Musset's 'Mardoche' should eclipse 'Albertus'.[23] Clearly, the poem's quality and effectiveness are primarily in its stylistic virtuosity: the author is only intermittently interested in the underlying philosophy—which is why this becomes somewhat ambiguous. Gautier seizes rather on each successive opportunity to indulge his fancy and deploy his already formidable verbal and technical skill. The visual element predominates in this 'monde où tout parle aux regards, où tout est poétique' (LXXVI); and, as Jasinski points out (*AR* 115), in 'les jeux d'ombre et de lumière, la profusion des couleurs, la saillie du détail', 'Albertus' transposes into literature the achievements of the new anti-Davidian school of painting. The death-knell of neo-classical poetry sounded by *Les Orientales* is spectacularly repeated here in an astonishing accumulation of details of striking intensity massed together: shape, number, size, contour, colour, texture, to create a powerful physical presence.

Apart from the visual element, Gautier's verbal intoxication is also given full rein. Poetry being for him essentially a process of deploying materials with a view to 'compasser des mots',

> D'enfiler dans un vers des mots, comme des perles
> Dans un cordon (L, LI)

certain virtuoso passages rely exclusively on the singularity of the individual components, where each term arrests eye and ear by a unique phonetic or plastic quality, producing a powerful cumulative effect:

> Cuchillos, kriss malais à lames ondulées,
> Kandjiars, yataghans aux gaines ciselées,
> Arquebuses à mèche, espingoles, tromblons,
> Heaumes et corselets, masses d'armes, rondaches . . . (LXXXVII)

> Stryges au bec crochu, Goules, Larves, Harpies,
> Vampires, Loups-garous, Brucolaques impies,
> Mammouths, Léviathans, Crocodiles, Boas . . . (CX)

The precise interpretation of the poem—assuming there is one at all—is not entirely clear, in spite of Gautier's quizzical assertion that his simple 'allegory' is self-evident (CXII). The hero follows Hamlet and the Byronic hero in having been unbalanced by an emotional trauma in the past which has made his ideal forever unrealisable. Death is therefore the sole escape from the torture of life's constant disillusion (LXXI, LXXIV). Partly out of curiosity, but largely from despair, the hero momentarily abandons painting, his only consolation (LXXXI), to betray the memory of his ideal (LXXXV) in surrender to physical temptation which brings ultimate destruction.

The subtitle, 'L'Ame et le péché, légende théologique', is ambiguous. Is a serious attempt at analysing a moral issue intended? Of what precise 'sin' is the hero guilty? Sainte-Beuve's assumption that the poem's lesson is one of 'le néant et le mensonge du plaisir'[24] is unconvincing, for as Jasinski has pointed out (cf. *AR* 116–19), Albertus is not deluded by sensuality. In selling his soul to the devil and surrendering to pleasure the hero is seeking not love, which he knows to be no longer possible, but oblivion; and in any case the author stresses his hero's innocence (LXXIV) rather than his guilty complicity. The only consistent argument seems to be that, given the nature of the ideal, by definition unattainable, the only course is to assume appearance is reality:

> —Jouissons, faisons-nous un bonheur de surface;
> Un beau masque vaut mieux qu'une vilaine face (LXXII).

But, the argument concludes, this conscious delusion is a supreme self-betrayal entailing the just punishment of damnation. If the poem is full of ambiguity, this is a reflection partly of Gautier's own moral waverings and partly of his impatience with abstract issues which keep him from purely aesthetic considerations.

It is, therefore, surely impossible to dismiss 'Albertus' in its entirety, as Faguet does[25] (along with most of Gautier's work) as 'vide', 'un pur rien', or to adopt Joanna Richardson's curious standpoint that it is 'unsuccessful' because 'the style continually distracts from the subject'.[26] A subject rarely interests Gautier unless its potentially 'distractive' element is great, unless, in other words, it provides scope for capricious development, skilful technical deployment and exploration of the mysterious ambiguities of existence. All these elements are offered by this archetypal romantic poem where style and subject are perfectly welded to create a boisterous, irrepressible, mock-heroic *tour de force*—but where, nevertheless, in spite of the bravado, the author's underlying malaise constantly breaks through.

La Comédie de la Mort (1838)

This, the second of the two volumes constituting the so-called 'Carlovingian cycle', was announced in 1835 but published only in February 1838. As with *Albertus* the general title covers both the title poem and a considerable number of 'Poésies Diverses')— this time fifty-six in all—composed since the appearance of *Albertus* in 1832, and with no semblance of unity or order. The temptation should be resisted to consider these miscellaneous poems of less value than the title poem merely because of their 'occasional' nature.

'La Comédie de la Mort'

The poem 'La Comédie de la Mort' is, like 'Albertus', inspired by what the self-deprecating Gautier termed his juvenile 'maladie gothique' (*SR* 13), and is as much a period piece as the earlier poem. This time, however, the tone is solemn and portentous, the element of facetiousness of 'Albertus' being replaced by a tense and at times moving subjectivity. The theme of death which in *Poésies* was limited to sparse and conventional treatment receives its first major analysis in this poem, and recurs from now on so insistently in Gautier's work that one critic has gone so far as to claim it to be 'sa pensée maîtresse'.[27]

Death held a morbid fascination for Gautier personally, over and above its obvious aesthetic potential and its pre-eminence in romantic preoccupations generally. Its spectacular exploitation by the poet's own favourite authors Ann Radcliffe, Young, Hervey, Goethe, Byron, Hoffmann and others was an additional recommendation to the deeply impressionable and melancholy Gautier. Moreover, the period was the heyday of European cemetery building, and evidence suggests that Gautier often frequented the Parisian cemeteries, then rapidly expanding (partly to cope with a succession of disastrous epidemics).[28] Gautier explicitly states that his poem was 'rêvé au Père Lachaise', a spot which, he admitted, like its companion, the Cimetière Montmartre, was calculated to plunge him into 'une mélancolie funèbre pour plusieurs jours' and to cause in him 'une invincible horreur, des moiteurs glacées dans le dos et des tressaillements nerveux' (*C* 163, 156, 157).

The treatment of the theme of death in Gautier, while conventionally 'romantic' in essence, is in some ways distinctive. Unlike the spiritual liberation seen in death expressed fervently by Lamartine or Hugo, death for Gautier is a plunge into a terrifying *néant*, a stifling and irreversible finality. If death is for Gautier an extinction, however, he is even more obsessed with what Baudelaire terms 'le vertige et l'horreur de néant' *(BOC* 698), and particularly with the agonising process of physical transformation that dying involves. Hence the gruesome depiction of corpses and graveyards where worms may be glimpsed acting out their lingering contribution to the process of decomposition which the dead continue physically to experience. Death is not only oblivion but 'le palpable néant' (IV); and it is no coincidence that in his appreciation of Baudelaire, and of Spanish painting, Gautier should overstress 'les verdeurs de la décomposition'.[29]

At the same time, the stock accessories of the macabre and of romantic necrophilia, already introduced into *Poésies* and 'Albertus', throng the pages of 'La Comédie de la Mort': skulls, skeletons, corpses, owls, yews, willows, will o' wisps in moonlit graveyards, coffins, black draperies and tombstones. Gautier never forgave Christianity for having surrounded death with mortifying horror (cf. *C* 156–7), and this opposition finds clear expression later in 'Bûchers et Tombeaux' *(EC)*. Yet he never ceased, as an artist, to relish the sheer plastic beauty and theatrical atmospherics of graveyard and vault where, with all her splendid insignia, 'la mort fait la coquette et prend un ton de reine' ('Portail').

The allegorical representation of death commonly chosen by Gautier is also distinctive. Death is no longer the fatal scytheman but a sensuous maiden, 'vierge aux beaux seins d'albâtre' (IX). Following the Italian sculptural tradition of Michelangelo, Bernini and Canova, renewed by nineteenth century funerary sculptors as represented in the Père Lachaise cemetery, Gautier portrays death in voluptuous, almost sexual terms, anticipating the further exploitation in this direction by the Pre-Raphaelites and Decadents.

Finally, because death is oblivion, Gautier follows generally the literary tradition which proclaims it as the definitive escape from life's torture, and those who welcome death in 'La Comédie de la Mort' are not so much (in spite of certain hints)[30] social failures as disappointed idealists cheated in their quest of the absolute, like Albertus himself.

Structurally the poem itself is somewhat confused, almost

inevitably so in view of its fragmented composition over five or six years (1831-6). The guiding argument remains clear, but is subordinated more than ever to the illustration and decoration of the idea. After an introductory personal meditation ('Portail') in which the poet confesses, in the sustained image of the gothic vault, his obsessive pessimism and proclaims the inescapability of death, the poem takes the form of an exploratory 'voyage sombre' (IX) to find the key to life's 'énigme funeste' (VIII). Starting from the realistic setting of the Père Lachaise cemetery on a raw wintry day and guided for part of the way by Death herself (a pallid maiden of haunting beauty), the poet undergoes a series of nightmarish hallucinations. The poem resolves itself into two sections of unequal length. The first, 'La Vie dans la Mort', poses (section I) the author's compulsive fear that the dead may not be really 'dead' and therefore insensible. Death may rather entail continued consciousness, coupled with a harrowing impotence exacerbated by the agony of being forgotten by the living. The state of death is characterised therefore not by the calm oblivion of traditional mythology but by 'impuissance et fureur'. This notion, 'idée dont j'ai ... toujours l'âme obsédée', is then illustrated by a double hallucination. First, the poet over-hears a dialogue between a still agonising corpse and the mocking worm intent on its gruesome yet natural activity (section II); and this episode is followed (III) by a further vision, this time experi-enced in the poet's own room, in which the tormented voice of Raphael, speaking through a death's head, curses the degenerate materialism of the nineteenth century, prophesying doom.

The second major section, the much longer 'La Mort dans la Vie', illustrates, by a series of variations on the theme, the proposition (section IV) that death is in the midst of life. There are those who carry 'l'invisible néant, la mort intérieure', constantly with them, who are spiritually dead; and indeed, inasmuch as disillusion is endemic to life, 'toute âme est un sépulcre où gisent mille choses'. This notion is then illustrated by what is in effect the climax of the entire poem, the successive interrogations of three key representatives of dissatisfied humanity as to their experience of life and their evaluation of the human condition: (V) Faust, (VI-VII) Don Juan, (VIII) Napoleon. Each shares a character of rebellious genius in various fields of human activity

—knowledge, pleasure and glory respectively—and their common experience is that of the disillusioned idealist: as 'martyrs de la pensée' (VI), each has been ultimately thwarted in his relentless search for the secret of life.

The poem concludes (section IX) with a personal meditation, exactly balancing in length the introductory 'Portail', which makes a final despairing plea to the life-giving forces of nature to ward off the ever-present menace of death.

In spite of its diffuseness, its often theatrical rhetoric, and its numerous borrowings of theme and detail, 'La Comédie de la Mort' has an undeniable majesty and power. The jaunty irony of 'Albertus' is replaced by a sombre, often moving eloquence, particularly evident in the direct confessional of the opening and closing passages. The allegorical figures themselves, in spite of their recurrence in general romantic mythology, have a certain complexity and resonance; they are particularly characteristic of the author and clearly voice Gautier's own despair.

The poem represents Gautier's nearest approach to the cosmic, philosophical vein of romanticism, and in some episodes, like the encounter with Napoleon's shade momentarily reanimated on the desolate Russian plain before plunging back into limbo, the poet achieves a starkly gruesome effect, anticipating the later apocalyptic inspiration of Hugo or Leconte de Lisle.

Finally, however, the impression which persists is of a welter of magnificent plastic imagery which risks at times submerging the thread of the argument. As Jasinski writes, 'L'idée se matérialise à l'extrême, se charge d'ornements factices ... l'effusion se fige un peu dans une perpétuelle traduction pittoresque et plastique'.[31] Tirelessly evoking the sensuous forms associated with the Christian concept of death—the gothic vaulting, the alabaster effigies, the sinuous draperies, the stained glass, the textured stone and the riot of architectural motifs—Gautier translates death into a curiously heady, voluptuous, almost exhilarating experience which diverts him momentarily from the gruesome reality and conveys his urgent plea for light over darkness, life over death.

'Poésies Diverses'

The body of miscellaneous poems accompanying, and unjustly

overshadowed by, the title poem 'La Comédie de la Mort' is remarkable for its great variety of inspiration, its technical mastery of different verse-forms in widely varying genres and the introduction, for the first time in Gautier's poetic career, of important new elements which turn away from the heady romanticism of 'Albertus' and 'La Comédie de la Mort' to announce the mature poet. Tonal and thematic unity are sacrificed to richness and diversity in this occasional poetry, composed over a period of several years.

Certainly much of the inspiration of these poems remains indistinguishable from that of 'La Comédie de la Mort'. These pieces were composed during the same turbulent period of Gautier's life; and in the magnificently sustained metaphysical pessimism of 'Thébaïde', 'Melancholia', 'Dédain', 'Après le Bal' and the 'prodigieuse symphonie', 'Ténèbres',[32] particularly, an impression is gained of a Gautier moving beyond fashionable romantic melancholy to a pathological state of apprehension, morbidity and even nihilism. The same significant allegorical figures of Faust, Goethe, Byron, Don Juan, Raphael, Hamlet and Napoleon recur to illustrate once more 'tous ces mots creux: amour, science et gloire' ('Thébaïde'). The gruesome dance of death recommences:

> Derrière nous le sol se crevasse et s'effondre.
> Nul ne peut retourner. Comme un maigre troupeau
> Que l'on mène au boucher, ne pouvant plus le tondre,
> La vieille Mob nous pousse à grand train au tombeau.
> ('Après le Bal')

The gloom is unrelieved and horrifying; Gautier is terrified at the thought of the artist's premature spiritual death, illustrated already in the title poem and now anticipated desperately in 'Le Trou du Serpent' and 'Thébaïde'. Often the pessimism assumes a direct, autobiographical form, a confession of the author's gnawing spiritual 'gangrène' ('Pensée de Minuit'), his obsession with remorseless Time ('Après le Bal') and reaching in 'Tristesse' a seeming finality of utter despair.

The entire volume is pervaded by this corrosive pessimism in which any external stimulant, however agreeable in itself, is liable to sullen or jaundiced interpretation. Thus an eighteenth century miniature exhales a haunting wistfulness ('Pastel'), a closed gate symbolises the what-might-have-been ('Watteau'), statues and paintings become sombre allegories of life's harshness ('Le Sphinx', 'Le Thermodon'), Paris is a tawdry prostitute ('Notre-Dame'), weeping Niobe becomes a cosmic figure ('Niobé'). Even art may be devalued, for

> J'ai regardé de près et la science et l'art:
> J'ai vu que ce n'était que mensonge et hasard.
> ('Thébaïde')

Beginning a poem ('A un Jeune Tribun') with thoughts of contrasting the supremacy of art with the vanity of the active life, the poet's original confidence turns sour, and the poem concludes that such value judgements are meaningless in face of the great leveller death.

This persistent despair is periodically offset by the celebration of art as sole refuge from life. True to his dictum that 'l'art est ce qui console le mieux de vivre' ('Préface', *Albertus*), Gautier turns to exult triumphantly in the great artistic models of the past: the astonishing achievement of Michelangelo ('Terza Rima', 'Cariatides'), Petrarch's mystic idealism ('Le Triomphe de Pétrarque'), the sublime naïvety of Dürer or of some more obscure German master, 'Raphaël inconnu' ('Melancholia', 'Magdalena'). Art can still create at will an exotic paradise ('Ce Monde-ci et l'autre') or recapture the enchanted world of the mediaeval tapestry ('A un Jeune Tribun'). And stifled in a 'decrepit' Europe ('Ce Monde-ci et l'autre'), already degraded by tourists ('La Chanson de Mignon') and brutalised by 'ce Paris bruyant et sale à faire peur' ('Le Premier Rayon de Mai'), the poet seeks the sanctuary of the mediaeval cathedral, 'pour me refaire au grand et me rélargir l'âme' ('Notre-Dame'). Again he delights in recomposing the visual world into an airy symphony of form, colour, texture and perfume ('Le Sommet de la Tour') or in creating an oasis of calm joy from some domestic interior ('Le Chant du Grillon'). Art thus sublimely redeems life's mediocrity ('Compensation'), suffusing its devotee with a simple pride and pleasure in his craft ('La Bonne Journée').

Apart from this dialectic between metaphysical despair and artistic rapture, two groups of short poems in the 'Poésies

Diverses' indicate an important evolution in Gautier's art: a ballad cycle, and a more diffuse group of imaginative transpositions of psychological or emotional states.

Essentially sentimental, nostalgic and melancholy, Gautier was naturally drawn to the ballad and romance genres both by temperament and artistic conviction, and he and Banville helped to renew contemporary interest in a hitherto neglected tradition in France, that of the folk song. The wistful beauty of legends of love and war, associated with an idealised, chivalric Middle Ages and persisting in vestiges of Italian, Spanish and Oriental song,[33] could not fail to attract the poet's romantic imagination. His aesthetic doctrine too, placing stress on apparent artlessness and naïvety, attracted him to the folk song. These qualities, already hinted at in *Poésies*, are united in this small group of romances ('Romance', 'Lamento', 'Les Papillons', 'Absence', 'Barcarolle', 'Tristesse', 'Villanelle Rythmique'), with their suggestion of personal loss (the premature death of a Doyenné favourite known as la Cydalise occurred in 1836) and their aura of pre-Verlainian nostalgia allied to a haunting, musical quality. In such pieces the allegedly unmusical Gautier captures something of that quality he praised in a Halévy melody, 'mélancolique . . . suave, douce et naive',[34] suggesting also a more penetrating resonance which inspired not only Monpou, the fashionable 'Berlioz de la ballade' (*HR* 258), but Berlioz himself.[35]

The last group of these 'Poésies Diverses', of unequal quality, comprises imaginative transpositions of varying human moods. Some, the least rewarding, convey thought by means of a too-explicit, somewhat laboured symbol, after the early romantic fashion ('La Chimère', 'Le Sphinx', 'Choc de Cavaliers', 'Le Pot de Fleurs', 'La Caravane', 'L'Hippopotame') and remain somewhat arid and pedestrian—though 'Niobé' and 'Versailles' are notable exceptions in the wider and subtler human significance they assume.

Others form a small group of exquisite madrigals in that strangely inconsequential manner which counts among Gautier's peculiar poetic achievements: such are the delicately *précieux* 'A deux beaux yeux' and the haunting 'Chinoiserie' and 'Sonnet' ('Pour veiner de son front . . .'). These beautiful poems are among the earliest expressions of the new vogue for things

Chinese which was so to fascinate later decades, a trend to which Gautier and, particularly, his daughter Judith, contributed much.

Finally, a varied series of short, imaginative tranpositions, already symbolist in their nuances and suggestivity, reminds us once again how unjust is the traditional view of an exclusively Parnassian Gautier: 'Le Spectre de la Rose', 'Les Colombes', 'Les Papillons', 'Rocaille', 'Pastel', 'Watteau', 'La Dernière Feuille'. Though the plastic imagination is still dominant, especially in the rococo sensibility of several of the poems, these pieces once more anticipate Verlaine in their subtlety, their naïvety and their wistfulness. It is arguable that these madrigals, ballads and transpositions of 'Poésies Diverses', too easily overshadowed by 'La Comédie de la Mort', constitute in fact Gautier's most successful and assured poetic compositions so far.

The collection *La Comédie de la Mort* as a whole offers, therefore, an astonishing richness of mood, genre and poetic technique (in its succession of sonnets, octosyllables, *terza rime*, pantoums, ballads and alexandrines), and attains a poetic quality hardly surpassed even in *Emaux et Camées* and *Dernières Poésies*, to which this volume looks forward. The fashionable Albertus is giving place to an assured artist intent on embroidering the dark canvas of life with his own distinctive 'fleurs du mal'. Only the forthcoming Spanish interlude will interrupt this poetic evolution for a while by offering him, in its revelation of lavish colour, the temptation to reanimate for almost the last time his flamboyant and moody romanticism.

THE MATURE POETRY, 1840–72

España (1845)

Published in 1845, *España* assembles together a disparate collection of forty-three miscellaneous poems composed mostly during or shortly after Gautier's journey through Spain during the summer of 1840. The motive for this journey was a practical one, spiced with an escapist spirit of adventure rather solemnly rationalised in the prefatory poem 'Départ'. The original instigator was Gautier's friend Eugène Piot, a wealthy dilettante from the Doyenné days who believed, wrongly as it transpired, that in a Spain still largely unsophisticated and recently ravaged by civil war (referred to incidentally in 'A la Bidassoa'), art treasures and antiques would be found in profusion and therefore acquired cheaply. On such an expedition Gautier's knowledge of art would be invaluable. The Frenchman Baron Taylor had, three years previously, attracted much attention by returning to France after an expedition to Spain officially commissioned by the king, Louis-Philippe, laden with a booty of over four hundred canvases. The immediate result of this had been the opening to the public, in 1838, of the Musée Espagnol in the Louvre.[36] Gautier was wildly enthusiastic over a project so perfectly calculated to dissipate the boredom of his sedentary existence ('J'étouffais à l'étroit dans ce vaste Paris', he confesses in 'Départ'), and the imaginative stimulus of such a journey would moreover, he believed, enable him to 'frapper un grand coup'[37] as a professional writer. Above all, the exotic allure of a Spain, still almost mediaeval, fraught with adventure and even danger, and familiarised through so many fashionable works, represented for any self-respecting romantic 'le pèlerinage par excellence, et comme la consécration suprême' (*JE* 6). For Gautier especially, born within sight of the Pyrenees and frequently contemptuous of France and its people, Spain was the revelation of a spiritual home, 'ma vraie patrie',[38] and long afterwards he recalled: 'Je me sentis là sur mon vrai sol et comme dans une patrie retrouvée' (*SR* 12).

Once again, little unity is apparent in this new volume. Despite the title, few of the pieces have any strongly recognisable Spanish character, and many are at best merely occasioned by stages in Gautier's itinerary and could have been composed in quite other surroundings. Yet the volume does nevertheless convey something of Gautier's fascination with Spanish art and culture and his deep, instinctive sympathy with certain aspects of the Spanish soul, besides reflecting his own continuing preoccupation with wider artistic and philosophical problems.

The properly Spanish poems of *España* include not merely those inspired by traditional Spanish subjects, like the accretion of myth around the legendary figures of the Cid and Boabdil ('Le Cid', 'Le Soupir du More') and which are either actual adaptations or pastiches of the *romancero*; but also those based on picturesque if conventional aspects of popular cultural tradition, like those which fuse music and dance ('Séguidille', 'Sérénade'). In the transcriptions of *coplas* especially Gautier captures something of the spirit of Spain as expressed in these traditional forms, notably the balance between gaiety and wistfulness, naïvety and sophistication, and he renews the *précieux* manner so often a feature of his art (cf. 'J'ai dans mon cœur', 'La Lune', 'J'ai laissé de mon sein de neige', 'Letrilla', 'J'allais partir'). Jasinski comments on Gautier's debt to popular culture in these poems, considering them 'les pièces les plus exquises peut-être du recueil' (*JE* 43).

Only accidentally or superficially Spanish is the group of poems inspired by aspects of Spanish art ('Saint Christophe d'Ecija', 'La Vierge de Tolède', 'Sainte Casilda'), architecture ('Perspective', 'L'Escurial'), or painting. The latter ('Ribeira', 'Sur le Prométhée de Madrid', 'Deux Tableaux de Valdès Léal', 'A Zurbaran') are perhaps the most significant, because of Gautier's tendency to interpret Spanish painting in a highly individual manner, overstressing its preoccupation with the morbid and violent. The canvases which most forcibly struck the poet's imagination on this expedition were not those expressing the sentimental charm of Murillo or the imperturbable mastery of Velasquez—both highly praised by him elsewhere—but rather the sadistic ferocity of a Ribera, the macabre side of a Zurbarán or a Valdés Leal, miscast by Gautier in the rôle of the 'Young de la peinture'; and from specific paintings of these artists Gautier produces striking transpositions completed by his own gloomy reflections on their 'étrange beauté' ('Ribeira').

The remainder of the pieces composing *España* are extremely diverse, alternating between the descriptive, the anecdotic and the contemplative, but with the poet's irrepressible fancy constantly to the fore. Some record impressions of scenes, sometimes with touches of neutral, objective realism dangerously close to matter-of-fact journalism. More usually, however, the apparently unexceptional is transformed by the poet's fanciful vision, a treatment involving hyperbole, heightened colouring, exaggerated responses or some unusual interpretation. Thus a Carthusian monastery assumes a forbidding, even sinister aspect ('En allant à la Chartreuse de Miraflorès', 'La Fontaine du Cimetière'), the royal palace becomes a livid monster ('L'Escurial'), a mountain ascent gives access to an eerie, cosmic landscape ('J'étais monté plus haut . . .'). The poet yields to a constant urge to polarise experience, and the tonality of the volume oscillates between the morbid (recurrence of themes of ennui, the cloister and death) and the voluptuous (themes of ecstasy: religious in 'Sainte Casilda', 'A Zurbaran', pantheistic in 'Les Yeux Bleus', amorous in 'Sérénade', 'Les Trois Grâces de Grenade').

Other poems celebrate particularly privileged features of Spain, like its exquisite flora ('La Petite Fleur rose', 'Le Laurier du Généralife'), or highlight its contrasting scenery, from its stark central wilderness ('In Deserto', 'J'étais monté plus haut') to its lush Andalusian gardens ('Le Laurier du Généralife') —and not forgetting the special magic of Spanish nights ('Les Trois Grâces de Grenade', 'Au Bord de la Mer').

Yet others prolong the vein of subjective, meditative romanticism and are, if at all, only tenuously Spanish. This was to be almost the last time Gautier treated wider philosophical or human problems in direct poetic form, either sustaining argument at length or compressing it sharply into vivid, symbolic form. These poems revive familiar romantic themes already exploited by Gautier himself. Compulsive meditations on mortality prolong the general tonality of 'La Comédie de la Mort' and should be read alongside the poems on the macabre aspects of Spanish art already referred to ('L'Horloge', 'Stances', 'En passant à Vergara', 'En passant près d'un cimetière' and the gruesome 'Les Affres de la Mort'). At the same time, declarations of Art for Art's Sake elitism stress once again the poet's unique but fatal divinity ('Le Pin des Landes', 'Consolation', 'Dans la Sierra', 'Le Poète et la Foule' and the mysterious 'Le Roi solitaire').

The diversity of *España* has led, as so often with Gautier's work, to the most partial or conflicting judgements. Contemporary views were as usual critical of the volume's borrowings and its subjectivity, while nevertheless applauding its grace and fancy. Later critics, however, claimed to detect in it the first manifestations of naturalism, a point overstressed by Brunetière[39] and taken up by Faguet and Lanson. The truth is rather that the poet sought and found in Spain not the objective truth of a neutral, impartial observer—Gautier was never that—but confirmation of ingrained romantic prejudices about its exotic or violent individuality. The result is a Spain tantalisingly incomplete, partially authentic yet stereotyped, visualised through the deforming prism of a poet's fancy and personality; a record, in fact, of intensely subjective reactions to certain selected aspects of the country: '*España* . . . n'est plus l'Espagne: elle en est l'intime résonance dans l'âme du poète . . .' (*JE* 36). Subjects and themes are thus constantly deformed, 'arranged' or romanticised to suit the artist's imaginative responses: the legendary taciturnity of Philip II symbolises the poet's own ennui ('Le Roi solitaire'), just as his palace is interpreted in accordance with prevailing romantic convention ('L'Escurial'). Even the actual details of a painting are unashamedly altered ('Sainte Casilda'). In this volume reality is therefore a transposed, not an actual reality, and the whole is still crowded with transcriptions of stock romantic models.

España is usually considered the transitional volume between the two phases of Gautier's poetic career. At this stage, notes Jasinski, 'sa poésie hésite entre des possibilités contraires: les brumes du nord s'y mêlent curieusement à la blonde lumière méridionale, le frisson à la joie, la méditation à la fantaisie légère' (*JE* 35). This antithesis is present throughout Gautier's entire work, but is perhaps particularly accentuated in this *recueil* which shares for the last time the sombre, confessional rhetoric of 'La Comédie de La Mort', yet foreshadows, particularly in a certain artistic realism allied to a fanciful romance form, the peculiar genre of the forthcoming *Emaux et Camées*. The final poem, 'Adieux à la Poésie', announces a break of almost five years of virtual poetic silence; and when *Emaux et Camées* is published in 1852, technique, form and content will be essentially different from the preceding volumes. *España* is still largely problematic poetry; *Emaux et Camées* will be essentially celebrative.

Emaux et Camées (1852)

Emaux et Camées, usually considered, somewhat unjustifiably, to be Gautier's supreme poetic achievement, was published on 17 July 1852 during the absence abroad of the author, touring the Middle East, and was greeted with almost universal acclaim. This first edition comprised only eighteen poems, but further editions successively enlarged this number until the last edition of Gautier's lifetime, the sixth, published in 1872, contained no less than forty-seven poems. Once again the volume has no thematic unity or structure, inevitable in the circumstances: composition of the individual poems of the 1872 edition ranged over a period of some twenty years (1849–68), and one poem indeed ('Plaintive Tourterelle') dates from as early as 1840; and each edition simply added 'new' poems at the end of the previous one, irrespective of subject or type. The disposition and order of the poems have therefore no significance, Gautier's only expressed wish being that 'L'Art' should be the concluding poem.[40] As all but four of the poems of the definitive edition are entirely composed in octosyllabic quatrains,[41] *Emaux et Camées* does however offer a formal unity lacking in the other *recueils*.

Gautier's choice of title, somewhat enigmatic at first glance, requires some comment. It reflects his abandonment, once for all, of the romantic ambition to create a kind of 'total' art, one of vast and profound ideological and philosophical pretensions which forces the emotional participation of the reader, in favour of a modest, reticent genre in which form rather than content is the overriding consideration. It is an art of the miniature, of 'petits sujets'[42] (recalling the *petits genres* of the Pléiade and the Précieux), rather than that of the broad canvas, a connoisseur art rather than an art of communication. The poet wishes to treat his subject neutrally, having sole regard to its artistic potential: the mummified hand of the murderer is as fascinating and as worthy, artistically, of contemplation as that of a beautiful woman ('Etude de Mains'); death, although intrinsically horrific, nevertheless offers irresistible aesthetic appeal ('Coquetterie Posthume', 'Bûchers et Tombeaux'). It is an art which attenuates without excluding feeling, which recalls Gautier's lifelong fascination with the arts of the miniaturist and the engraver, and which abandons the three-dimensional to concern itself primarily with the craftsman's exploration of physical contour:

Ce titre, *Emaux et Camées*, exprime le dessein de traiter sous forme restreinte de petits sujets, tantôt sur la plaque d'or ou de cuivre avec les vives couleurs de l'émail, tantôt avec la roue du graveur de pierres fines, sur l'agate, la cornaline ou l'onyx ... (*HR* 322).

Just as the hero of *Mademoiselle de Maupin* had revelled in his 'songes de pierre' (*MM* 209), so here the profusion of precious stones and minerals conveys an intensely personal vision of life seen at a remove, transposed into a symphony of rare substances. Reality is explored plastically: Gautier's 'cameos' are 'sculptés dans l'agate des mots',[43] for

Il est doux, pour une âme que n'altère pas l'âpre soif du gain, de *ciseler* solitairement dans le marbre et dans les vers, ces deux matières dures, étincelantes et froides, son rêve d'amour et de beauté . . . [44]

Gautier's title, therefore, testifies strikingly to the evolution in poetic taste from an effusive, introspective romanticism to more succinct, crystalline forms:

Les Emaux, les Camées, les Cariatides, les Festons, les Astragales, les Améthystes, les choses peintes, gravées, sculptées, dessinées, remplacent dans les titres des recueils poétiques les Voix, les Chants, les Méditations, les Harmonies, les Consolations, les Pensées, et tous épanchements de l'âme. Tout est plastique et pittoresque.[45]

Typifying the new spirit, Gautier proclaimed: 'La plastique est l'art supérieur',[46] noting blandly 'le calme est à la mode aujourd'hui' (*HR* 364). *Emaux et Camées* represents the natural culmination of these trends.

Plasticism also implies escapism, and the entire volume triumphantly exemplifies the artist's rejection of *engagement* announced in the simple introductory statement of 'Préface'. Faced with the agitations of 1848 and tragically disappointed in his hopes for an artistic revival with the new régime, the poet follows his model, Goethe, in abdicating all social responsibility and withdrawing into a private world.[47] Further, the word 'médaillon' which Gautier used of the genre of *Emaux et Camées*[48] implies the notion of selecting individual objects, animate or inanimate, for transposition into purely aesthetic, stylised miniatures and thus the reducing of life to 'a sort of museum for private contemplation',[49] narrowed still further by the dispassionate vehicle of the octosyllabic quatrain.

The deceptive appearance of sameness presented by the successive quatrains hides an extraordinary richness and diversity of inspiration and mood. Most representative perhaps is the group of varied love poems which, as so often with Gautier, take the form not of passionate, direct statements but of elaborate, decorative *médaillons*. Such poems convey, as Baudelaire noted perceptively of *Mademoiselle de Maupin*, 'non pas la fureur de l'amour, mais la *beauté* de l'amour et la *beauté* des objets dignes d'amour . . .',[50] and pay oblique, almost incidental homage to a series of emotional attachments of uncertain intensity. They range in mood from amused ingenuity exploiting whimsical, *précieux* imagery ('Les Accroche-Cœurs') to a direct and poignant simplicity expressing his love for Carlotta ('Dernier Vœu', 'La Fleur qui fait le Printemps'). Some are light fantasies already foreshadowing Verlaine, conveying the tremulousness of love ('Odelette Anacréontique') or its bitter-sweet quality ('Carnaval de Venise', IV), yet with that delicate irony with which Gautier usually chose to invest this diversion: 'Il parle, ce ne sont que madrigaux, galanteries parfumées en beau style précieux'.[51] In other poems, nature's fragility conveys extravagant homage ('La Rose-Thé'), or the poet may revive the conventions of the mediaeval romance ('Plaintive Tourterelle').

In others, the object of the poet's admiration is a mere pretext for decorative transposition or thematic variation. The heroine herself is virtually absent, and only close reading reveals that 'Affinités Secrètes', 'Symphonie en blanc majeur' and 'Premier Sourire du Printemps' are indeed madrigals at all. The poet may, in an allusive *divertissement*, pursue his feminine ideal (cf. 'La Nue') through its various cosmopolitan incarnations ('Le Poème de la Femme'). 'Affinités Secrètes', applying pseudo-science to salon *préciosité*, attains a peculiar resonance, completely eluding classification. Yet in spite of the decorative, ceremonious approach to love in these poems and the tendency to woo by proxy, the theme of desire is modulated in a variety of registers: provocatively erotic ('Carmen', 'Inès de las Sierras'), mock-heroic ('Rondalla'), delicately sensual ('A une Robe rose'), fatal ('Cærulei Oculi', 'Etude de Mains'), wistfully retrospective ('Carnaval de Venise', IV).

Preferring museums to 'life', 'la statue à la femme et le marbre à la chair' (*SR* 6), Gautier often needed the stimulus of some existing artefact to spur creation. The incidence of artistic inspiration, provoking the characteristic *transposition d'art*, is greater than ever in *Emaux et Camées*, and attests the range of Gautier's experience in various media. As already in *España*, the poet may work directly from precise canvases (a Canaletto and a Tiepolo in 'Carnaval de Venise', Correggio in 'La Nue', several masters in 'Le Poème de la Femme'), from water-colours ('Le Souper des Armures', 'La Fellah', 'Les Néréides'), or from etchings ('Vieux de la Vieille', a Goya in 'Bûchers et Tombeaux'). Alternatively, inspiration may come from sculpture ('Contralto', 'Le Poème de la Femme', 'A une Robe rose', 'Fantaisies d'Hiver'), from music ('Carnaval de Venise', 'Contralto') or from literature itself ('Carmen', 'Inès de las Sierras'). But most poems reveal composite sources: 'Vieux de la Vieille' merges eye-witness accounts of a topical event with reminiscences from literature (Heine, Sedlitz) and from art (Raffet), while 'Le Souper des Armures' fuses a drama of Hugo, an English water-colour, and various diffuse legendary sources.[52]

The *transposition* technique is, therefore, far from straightforward. The haunting 'Carnaval de Venise', for example, moves easily from its original Paganini air rooted in the realistic setting of a suburban open-air café through an elaborate series of 'variations' in which the melodic, the painterly (Tiepolo, Canaletto) and the theatrical (the Italian *Commedia dell'Arte*) all participate before concluding in a Verlainian *fête galante*.

The above may nevertheless be considered 'simple' transpositions in that they are largely descriptive and directly allusive. There are however more subtle transpositions, involving a transference of sense perception. For in this visionary world everything obeys the cosmic law of metamorphosis. Matter itself is interchangeable, the apparently static is elusive:

> Marbre, perle, rose, colombe,
> Tout se dissout, tout se détruit;
> La perle fond, le marbre tombe,
> La fleur se fane et l'oiseau fuit.
>
> . . .
>
> Par de lentes métamorphoses,
> Les marbres blancs en blanches chairs,
> Les fleurs roses en lèvres roses
> Se refont dans des corps divers.
> ('Affinités Secrètes')

To convey this universal mobility the senses constantly merge and interact: '. . . mon caprice qui persiste . . . se transpose, . . .

passant de la forme au son . . .' ('Contralto'). Thus individual metaphors transfer from the auditive to the visual: 'la gamme monte en fusée' ('Carnaval de Venise') or, vice versa, the visual may evoke music ('Contralto'). The most striking example of sensual 'correspondences' is the complex series of transpositions of 'Carnaval de Venise': here, Gautier hears the music and *sees* it simultaneously, transposed visually into the minims, quavers, trills and arpeggios of the stave—before all becomes whimsically animated. Many phrases acquire an indefinable, mysterious resonance: 'de blancs secrets', 'la brume sonore', 'spleen lumineux', 'des conversations fleuries', 'lumineusement noir', 'arabesques d'or'.

The poet 'pour qui le monde extérieur existe' is clearly conscious of the mystery and ambiguity of the universe of appearance, conscious of an ambivalence already suggested a few years previously by his experience with drugs, when 'mon ouïe s'était prodigieusement développée, j'entendais le bruit des couleurs. Des sons verts, rouges, bleus, jaunes, m'arrivaient par ondes parfaitement distinctes'.[53] 'Affinités Secrètes' alone, with its solemn and mysterious parallelisms and its continuous transmutation of matter and spirit, illustrates Gautier's profound awareness that surface reality is not explicit. One recalls in this context Baudelaire's praise of Gautier's 'immense intelligence innée de la *correspondance* et du symbolisme universels' (*BOC* 689), which in turn has led certain modern critics to stress Gautier's affinity with the Symbolist school.[54]

The poet's awareness of this spiritual, mystical dimension is, however, intermittent, and *Emaux et Camées* contains much precise documentation of external reality, including the humble and the sordid. Gautier enjoyed a reputation among his contemporaries as a 'modern', and he is aware of the picturesque potential of contemporary subjects, which present a special artistic challenge:

Il faut encourager ces tentatives très difficiles et qui exigent le goût le plus délicat, d'amener à la forme poétique les choses de la vie actuelle, nos mœurs, nos habitudes, nos fêtes, nos tristesses en habit noir . . . (*HR* 377).

In the discreet evocations of the fashionable milieux of the demi-mondaines, of formal garden or embassy ball, of the *bals masqués* of the Second Empire, of Garnier's Opéra with its new Rossini or latest Verdi, Gautier suggests the continuance under Louis-Philippe and Napoleon III of the worldly elegance of an earlier courtly tradition in which woman remains the arbitress of taste and the sole surviving symbol, in nineteenth century urban France, of eternal beauty. The Cydalise is a reincarnation of the Pompadour ('Le Château du Souvenir'), just as the poet recognises in Madame Sabatier the symbol of ancient classical beauty living on in the present ('Apollonie').

But it is not only the fashionable pleasure-seeking world which is recorded in *Emaux et Camées*, for 'la poésie, toute fille du ciel qu'elle est, n'est pas dédaigneuse des choses les plus humbles' ('Préface', *Les Jeunes-France*). In graphic reportage the ordinary, workaday world is also glimpsed: the world of attics and chimney pots ('La Mansarde'), of blind beggars ('Carnaval de Venise', 'L'Aveugle'), of grimy boats ('Tristesse en Mer'), of the suburban café ('Carnaval de Venise'). Such scenes compose a series of fragmented *tableaux parisiens*, depicting the courtesan flirting in her carriage, bourgeois politicians en route for the Chambre, the polluted, murky Seine, the irreverent sparrows ('Nostalgies d'Obélisques'). Finally, to such external realism correspond touches of psychological realism: a disabused lucidity ('Le Monde est méchant'), the realisation that life is onerous ('Après le Feuilleton') or just prosaic ('La Mansarde'), the sardonic judgement passed on 'ce peuple impie et fou' ('Nostalgies d'Obélisques').

The world of nature inspires another group of varied poems, the poet's approach to nature being fundamentally similar to that, already characterised by *Poésies*, of purely artistic exploitation. It is true that, whenever it suits him, Gautier can adopt a more conventional approach, as in the direct lyricism of 'La Fleur qui fait le Printemps', or the therapy implied in 'Premier Sourire du Printemps', where nature's unsullied delicacy accuses man's restless degeneracy. Usually, however, the natural world is subjected to the poet's transforming fancy through a process identical to that operating in his semi-autobiographical hero Tiburce in 'La Toison d'Or':'à force de vivre dans les livres et les peintures, il en était arrivé à ne plus trouver la nature vraie'. Gautier's natural world ceases, in fact, to be 'natural': use is constantly made of his most recurrent poetic tricks to heighten and enhance the vegetable world which basically he found devoid of interest—the devices of allegory, symbol and personification. Humanisation is an almost automatic process too: fountains weep, swallows converse, flowers beckon. The most characteristic of the nature poems are those which create a fairyland of delicate decorative motifs around the two privileged seasons for Gautier, spring with its special magic ('Premier Sourire du Printemps', 'La Fleur qui fait le Printemps') and the stark tracery of winter ('Fantaisies d'Hiver'). Nature orchestrates her charms in a triumphant and coquettish display, selecting from her 'palette' her spectacular floral magic, 'ses feux d'artifice de fleurs', her 'tuniques pourpres' and 'couronnes d'or', to enthrall the poet-aesthete. Each flower is magnificently unique: the delicate tea rose, the tulip 'au port superbe', the daisy, 'belle de sa parure agreste', the lily 'par l'aube argenté'. Gautier reverses the traditional standpoint: it is not art which models itself on nature, but 'la nature, de l'art jalouse' ('Le Château du Souvenir'), which attempts consciously to elevate itself into art. Nature is thus constantly seen through the prism of the poet's peculiar vision: as Sainte-Beuve commented of the poet, 'sa manière est une *manière* s'il en fut jamais; mais elle est bien à lui, et il s'y joue'.[55]

Lastly, in this reputedly impassive, austere volume in which, supposedly, 'le poète est absent de son œuvre',[56] it is perhaps still necessary, following Maxime du Camp's stress on the directly personal inspiration of much of this collection (op. cit., p. 175), to insist how subjective and lyrical are inspiration and expression. Jasinski in turn has enumerated some of the most directly personal and moving of these external sources—elusive emotional attachments, the crushed hopes of the aftermath of 1848, escape to the self-contained world of art—which are condensed into these short pieces whose very tightness of structure prevents effusiveness (cf. *PC*, I, LXXXIX, XCII). Many of the poems are profoundly elegiac, reflecting, often directly and poignantly, the poet's dejection and his desire to escape ('Ce que disent les Hirondelles'), his hopeless love for Carlotta ('Dernier Vœu', 'La Fleur qui fait le Printemps'), his ennui ('Nostalgies d'Obélisques'), the 'cercle d'enfer' of relentless journalism and social slander which sour life ('Après le Feuilleton', 'Le Monde est méchant'), his grieving for the irretrievable past ('Le Château du Souvenir') which makes the volume a veritable 'musée du souvenir'.[57] Above all, the passing of time has accentuated the poet's sombre premonitions of death. Although he can still celebrate its strange beauty in either its Christian or pagan rituals ('Coquetterie Posthume', 'Bûchers et Tombeaux'), its inexorability strikes indifferently at both old ('Vieux de la Vieille') and young (the acutely poignant 'Les Joujoux de la Morte')—as indeed it awaits the poet himself ('Dernier Vœu'), filling his morbid imagination with visions of rites and *danses macabres* ('Bûchers et Tombeaux'). The very age itself seems disintegrating: the war heroes, vestige of an irrecoverable grandeur, inspire the gloomy reflection:

> Ils furent le jour dont nous sommes
> Le soir et peut-être la nuit.
> ('Vieux de la Vieille')

Art alone represents the sole possible human triumph over the forces of negation which suffocate man, and 'La Nue' and 'Le Merle' once more give fervent expression to Gautier's fundamental idealism, periodically shaken as he contemplates contemporary disharmony and contrasts it with pagan antiquity:

> Le squelette était invisible
> Au temps heureux de l'Art païen;
> L'homme, sous la forme sensible,
> Content du beau, ne cherchait rien.
> ('Bûchers et Tombeaux')

The openly didactic 'L'Art', written as reply to Banville's *odelette* 'A Théophile Gautier' and not really integrated into *Emaux et Camées*, reconciles, as Jasinski points out, the poet's faith in Parnassian virtues with less austere, more capricious forces: 'Si [la pièce] prêche une fermeté dont pourra se réclamer le Parnasse, elle sauvegarde aussi "le rêve flottant", non sans affinités avec le symbolisme' (*PC*, I, cxxix). The poem is a lucid statement of general aesthetic (as opposed to purely poetic) principle; and while its precise application to the content of *Emaux et Camées* remains debatable it illustrates Gautier's stress on the plastic nature of the different arts (poetry, music, sculpture and painting respectively), as well as their common allegiance to so-called 'Parnassian' principles. The poem focuses specifically on two concepts: that form alone can perpetuate the insubstantial 'rêve flottant' and so alone can conquer man's condition of mortality; and that this achievement is only possible through patient and laborious struggle over refractory matter and by resisting the temptation to facility. The integrity of the artist as craftsman is a prerequisite of that excellence which alone ensures permanence.

These brief comments do not of course do justice to the variety and skill of this rich and complex volume. With its multiple echoes it is at the meeting point of so many literary and artistic trends. Looking backwards, in a poem like 'Le Souper des Armures' with its momentary reanimation of the gothic impedimenta of 'Albertus', it also looks forward towards the later symbolist aesthetic. *Emaux et Camées* is not adequately characterised by any single 'Art for Art's Sake' or other formula: the best of its poems elude any glib classification. Even the impression of simple artlessness is calculated, as a glance at the many variants will show. The unassuming ease of the octosyllable is deceptive, concealing the virtuosity of an assured craftsman in full possession of his resources, triumphantly overcoming the challenge of this unprepossessing yet demanding metrical form.

Dernières Poésies (1872)

The posthumous miscellany *Dernières Poésies* (the title is not Gautier's; cf. *PC* I, xv), assembling a considerable residue of poems, ranges in content from early pieces (for example, the important 'Ode' to Jean Duseigneur, contemporary with 'Albertus') to unfinished fragments composed shortly before the poet's death in 1872. Varying in both quality and genre, the volume includes meditative *transpositions d'art* ('A Ernest Hébert: Le Banc de Pierre', and the striking 'L'Ombre de Dieu'); various untypical attempts at official pieces celebrating public events ('Le 28 Juillet'); facetious poetic exercises like the amusing 'Epître monorime' to Charles Garnier, comprising seventy verses composed on a single rhyme; pastiches like the ingenious mock *romancero* 'Allitérations'; and the moving elegy 'Le Glas intérieur', composed on the death of the poet's mother in 1848 and which he refrained from publishing during his lifetime.

The more frivolous genres represented here should not be

entirely dismissed; they are a characteristic aspect of the poet's art. They recall the importance Gautier attached to poetic virtuosity and the gift of improvisation, to the concept of the *difficulté vaincue* already noted, to the challenge of preconceived formal structures, and to the indifference to subject-matter ('Sur une Boucle d'Oreille' pays homage to an earring, 'Le Navet' to a cooking recipe!). In general, they triumphantly illustrate Gautier's key principle of art as play.

An illustration is provided by the series of *bouts-rimés*, an exercise at which Gautier was an acknowledged master. The poet composed some of these in Princess Mathilde's salon, on pre-arranged rhyme-schemes, within a limited time, as Bergerat recalls of the sonnet 'Estelle': 'Nous allâmes une fois jusqu'à lui proposer le problème effroyable d'un sonnet-bout-rimé-acro-stiche, avec sujet imposé: en un quart d'heure, il fit une merveille' (*EB* 98). One such poem, addressed to the Princess, is significantly signed 'Son bouffon Gautier'—a revealing comment on Gautier's attitude both socially and artistically.

The collection of *Dernières Poésies* as a whole is, however, dominated artistically by its magnificently accomplished series of sonnets dedicated to Gautier's many friends: Ingres, Hébert, Popelin, Maxime du Camp, Madame de la Grangerie and his patron the Princess, while others reflect his love for Victorine, Marie Mattei and Carlotta Grisi. Gautier's esteem for the sonnet has already been noted (see above, p. 26), and in this se-quence it is evident that the poet is consciously considering the nature of the sonnet form. Apart from several uses of the term itself ('tu veux un sonnet' in 'Trop modeste est ton vœu', 'ce sonnet pieux' in 'L'Ombre de Dieu', 'un sonnet plein d'art' in 'Modes et Chiffons'), he is aware of the historical associations of the form and implies its particular appropriateness to the madrigal genre ('Trop modeste'), and its traditional links with *préciosité* ('Modes et Chiffons'). A strikingly original piece is the third sonnet to Popelin entitled simply 'Le Sonnet', a complex transposition which attempts ingeniously to externalise in a scene of mediaeval chivalry the technical progression of the sonnet from the sedate opening quatrain, represented by armoured knights, through a quickening tempo to the more sprightly decorative tercet depicting the pages fussing round their mistress.

It is in the sequence of amorous sonnets that Gautier is seen at his most characteristic and inventive. These take the form of the 'médaillon' or 'pur profil moderne' already defined by the author in connection with *Emaux et Camées*, and present affinities with the traditional *précieux* diversion of the *blason* or Marino's 'galleries'. Here, Gautier attains a density and resonance in striking individual verses of haunting beauty.

In the Marie Mattei cycle the theme of modernity is uppermost: 'J'aimais autrefois . . .' explicitly rejects the classical for the contemporary ideal. Consequently, traditional mythology is replaced by a heroine who, dressed by the fashionable *couturières* of the day, enjoys intimate tea parties, smoking and amorous excursions by cab to the Bois de Boulogne.

Not that the poet, cosmopolitan as ever, is insensible to less contemporary ideals of beauty. As we have seen, beauty for Gautier was composed of a transient, relative aspect and an eternal, immutable one, and several of these poems celebrate not the particularised, realistic heroine of the Marie Mattei cycle or the composite, exotic ideal of 'Parfois une Vénus . . .' but a serene, hieratic ideal of Parnassian gravity at times attaining an almost cosmic quality. The beautiful 'La Tulipe', an early poem, elevates Victorine's complex beauty into a kind of rich, heraldic majesty, the solemn 'L'Impassible' presents a daunting yet mysterious infinity, while 'Sur une Boucle d'Oreille' sets Carlotta against a stellar backcloth of the night sky and the wheeling systems.

Nowhere is Gautier's madrigal formula more triumphantly displayed than in the cycle of fifteen late sonnets dedicated in homage to his patron Princess Mathilde. Understandably, the character of this cycle, as opposed to the muted realism of the Marie Mattei sequence, is essentially that of the courtly, Platonic apotheosis of love ('La Vraie Esthétique', 'Les Déesses posent'). All the traditional features are present: the quintessential perfection of the heroine-Goddess, her omnipresence yet remoteness, her benevolent humanity yet also her insubstantiality and inviolability. The poet is the obsequious 'rêveur obscur':

> Que peut le ver rampant pour l'étoile sereine,
> Le caillou pour la perle et l'ombre pour le jour?
> ('L'Etrenne du Poète')

The prostrate devotee offers his unworthy verse in sacrificial homage ('Sonnet Dédicace', 'L'Etrenne du Poète), envious of the intimacy of light and air with the object of his cult ('Baiser rose, Baiser bleu').

Nothing illustrates Gautier's Art for Art's Sake principles more eloquently than these poems. In the shadow of a war which was to destroy the ageing poet and his world (cf. 'Le Vingt-Sept mai'), each of these exquisite pieces records and elaborates a frivolous non-event: a posed portrait, a birthday, a minute scratch on a bare shoulder, the interplay of light and textured material, a delicate ankle emerging from a hem. They represent a kind of visual *marivaudage* in which pagan mythology, modern realism, details of jewels, textures and colour are interwoven into miniature symphonies of rococo fantasy in which, once more, sensory correspondences play an integral part.

The sonnet sequences of *Dernières Poésies* present the climax of that art of the madrigal so characteristic of Gautier. Freed at last, by the kindness of his patron, from material cares and more than ever contemptuous of contemporary preoccupations, Gautier's art achieves here, in the taut intricacy of the sonnet, its full and mature expression as his fancy and idealism deploy themselves freely in that private, self-contained and exclusive world of art. The density and rigidity of the sonnet form counteract the temptation—not always resisted in *Emaux et Camées*—to pedestrianism and prolixity.

Yet despite this tautness, like the best of *Emaux et Camées* many of these poems, almost casually, prolong thought beyond the immediate context. Certainly they speak of the rare beauty of external form; but they hint also at the essential ambiguities of appearance and reality. The poet is more than ever aware of the fluidity and inherent mystery of this world of forms and of its relationship to that elusive private world which the true artist seeks but can never quite find. As Keats's urn teased him out of thought, so Gautier gazes entranced towards the unattainable 'profil perdu':

> A l'art exquis, s'ajoute le mystère,
> Le Sphinx coquet irrite le désir.
> ('Le Profil Perdu')

IV

OTHER WORKS

TRAVEL

Paradoxically the essentially sedentary and indolent Gautier was also an inveterate traveller whose life and work were periodically nourished with rich cosmopolitan material. That he should have become so is perhaps something of an accident. Until 1840 the self-confessed 'Parisien complet' had only been tempted to stray across the French border a few miles by Nerval's enthusiasm, in the friends' youthful escapade into Holland and Belgium in 1836; and even then, he admits, 'je restai bien 3 mois à me décider à ce voyage de 15 jours'.[1]

Yet the sense of adventure and lure of the exotic were innate in the Gautier whose favourite childhood reading had been *Robinson Crusoe* and *Paul et Virginie*. His early autobiographical hero d'Albert confessed 'avec quelle avidité je dévore les romans et les histoires de voyages' (*MM* 62), and the sheer excitement of foreign travel is well caught in the verve of Gautier's first travelogue, 'Un Tour en Belgique et en Hollande' (in *Caprices et Zigzags*).

But it was the revelation of Spain in 1840 which, releasing him from disillusion and routine in Paris, confirmed and deepened his *wanderlust*: 'Depuis, je n'eus d'autre idée que de ramasser quelque somme et de partir; la passion ou la maladie du voyage s'était développée en moi'.[2] An intimate of Gautier could therefore write later, without exaggeration, that 'les voyages avaient été la grande passion de Gautier', and recount the poet's acute disappointment at not being accepted as a member of an official French delegation to visit China.[3]

The prime motive for Gautier's travel writing was ostensibly to provide straightforward, informative and well-documented eye-witness accounts of life and scenes abroad for the French public; and although these terms of reference were elastic, credit must be given him for the pains he took to fulfil this mission conscientiously. At the very outset of his career as a travel writer he condemned those who deformed reality by romanticising their travels, pointedly cautioning the reader that 'Il n'y aura dans ma relation que ce que j'aurai vu avec mes yeux'.[4] Thus he claims his *Voyage en Espagne* to be the 'relation consciencieuse' (*VE* 276), composed of 'des descriptions de l'exactitude la plus scrupuleuse' (*VE* 106), of a 'touriste descripteur et daguerréotype littéraire' (*VE* 149). Similarly, the purpose of *Constantinople*, he claims, is to inform, not to indulge in speculative fancy: 'Je ne parle que de ce que j'ai vu' (*C* 44). Leaving Venice he suppresses a momentary qualm that he might have done more to instruct the reader: 'Dieu sait si nous avions fait en conscience notre métier de voyageur' (*VI* 292).

Gautier declares that the first task of the travel writer is to instruct by close observation of 'ces mille petites différences qui avertissent qu'on a changé de pays', seizing on the details of raw life 'tracés sur le vif' (*VI* 295), and he brought to this task an insatiable curiosity and, above all, an obsessive and fastidious vision which he himself humorously records:

En six semaines, nous avions usé trois lorgnons, abîmé une jumelle, perdu une longue-vue. Jamais personne ne se livra à une pareille débauche d'oeil. Nous regardions quatorze heures par jour sans nous arrêter . . . (*VI* 292–3)

Consequently, Gautier's writings are much more than an aesthete's impressions of paintings and architecture, even when, as in *Voyage en Russie*, his immediate purpose is to gather artistic material; and no detail or aspect of life is too humble or insignificant to be faithfully recorded.

Dutifully, personal digressions are uncompromisingly controlled: 'Nous n'en abusons pas', he reassures the reader (*VR* 71).[5] Indeed, for the modern reader this discretion is taken too far: one would have welcomed details of personal contacts—not to mention some record of his known emotional entanglements in Spain and Italy. But Gautier is adamant: 'Raconter ses aventures, c'est de la fatuité: raconter celles des autres, c'est de l'indiscrétion' (*VI* 296).

It is nevertheless clear that, intent as Gautier is on escaping through travel 'la civilisation, mon ennemie mortelle' (*VE* 364) with the adulterated values of 'cette prosaïque et malencontreuse année 1840' (*VE* 137), his narratives fall short of the total objectivity he claimed for them. Such psychological interference inevitably colours his responses. His eye, unerring in seizing meticulous detail, is nevertheless selective: like many tourists abroad, Gautier seeks confirmation of certain ingrained prejudices. Everything has a tendency to become a stick with which to beat contemporary degeneracy, particularly the magnificent achievements of Spanish, Venetian and classical Greek art, all symbols of an irrecoverable grandeur.[6]

It was one of Gautier's axioms that the conscientious traveller should visit a country at its most 'characteristic' season: 'Nous sommes d'avis qu'il faut visiter les pays dans leur saison violente: l'Espagne en été, la Russie en hiver' (*VE* 180). Again, he recalls later, 'aux mois les plus torrides de l'année, je visitai toute l'Afrique française' (*SR* 12). This courageous principle reveals a significant aspect of Gautier's approach to travel: the tireless search for the 'characteristic', particularly for local colour in its more bizarre aspects. He is constantly caught testing reality against pre-conceived personal visions of certain 'patries idéales' which the poet-dreamer 'fait habiter par ses rêves' (*VI* 65). Just as in 1836 Nerval and he had sought in Holland the Rubens type, so in Spain 'nous espérions trouver là le type espagnol féminin' (*VE* 29), while the real Venice is measured against 'la Venise de Canaletto, de Bonnington' (*VI* 71). In consequence, examples not satisfying his personal preconceptions are liable to be summarily dismissed, and disappointment is often in store; in Spain he is even led to conclude: 'Ce que nous entendons en France par type espagnol n'existe pas' (*VE* 92).[7] Conversely, the most intense pleasure of all comes when dream and reality momentarily coincide: 'Rencontrer dans la réalité ce qui jusqu'alors n'a été pour vous que costume d'Opéra et dessin d'album, est une des plus vives impressions que l'on puisse éprouver en voyage' (*LP* 23).

The usual tourist addiction to the quaint, the picturesque and the spectacular is everywhere evident. As a 'jeune Français enthousiaste et romantique', a 'pauvre voyageur épris de couleur locale' (*VE* 30, 31), Gautier is apt to confuse eccentricity with originality and to overpraise any triumphant persistence of local tradition, legend or folk-lore in the face of the tide of modern uniformity which, he believed, was about to engulf the world:

C'est un spectacle douloureux pour le poète, l'artiste et le philosophe, de voir les formes et les couleurs disparaître du monde, les lignes se troubler, les teintes se confondre et l'uniformité la plus désespérante envahir l'univers sous je ne sais quel prétexte de progrès (*VE* 210).

Thus the bullfight, the gondola, the dervish and the gipsy all merit lengthy and fervent descriptions as being uniquely characteristic of national culture, and Gautier prides himself, moreover, on identifying physically with each experience, sweltering in the arena in Madrid, lounging in a gondola on the Grand Canal, squatting cross-legged devouring Turkish Delight—all 'par amour pour la couleur locale' (*C* 98).

It would nevertheless be grossly misleading to imply that Gautier's travelogues are composed of facile, conditioned responses to the over-obvious tourist attractions. Within the limits of an exuberant and idealistic nature his spirit is uncompromisingly independent. He frequently goes out of his way to attack prevalent clichés. In Milan, after describing the usually-quoted tourist opinion of the main square, he comments: 'Nous ne sommes pas de cet avis', and explains why (*VI* 46). He does not hesitate to write of Florence: 'L'aspect général . . . contrairement à l'idée qu'on s'en fait, est triste' (*VI* 337). Certainly the well-trodden tourist paths are covered: the bridge at Avignon, St Mark's Square, the Kremlin, the Parthenon, the Alhambra; but there is much more that the indefatigable and painstaking Gautier records. Well aware of the dangers of falling into the tourist trap he wrote:

. . . nous aimons connaître des villes autre chose. que la physionomie officielle, dessinée, décrite, racontée partout, et nous sommes curieux, le légitime tribut d'admiration payé, de soulever ce masque monumental que chaque cité se pose sur le visage pour dissimuler ses laideurs et ses misères (*VI* 281).

Accordingly, he evolves his own method of visiting a strange town, based on the principle of dispensing with an official guide ('ne haïssant rien tant que les *cicerone* de profession' (*LP* 32), and relying on instinct and chance, since 'le hasard est le meilleur guide' (*VE* 102). The resulting spectrum of life is consequently much wider and more authentic than that suggested by the official façade, and the less salubrious districts claim some attention: the old town of Algiers, St Petersburg's 'quartier de haillons', the maze of back streets of Constantinople's bazaar. An important quality of Gautier's travelogues is revealed here: they are consciously improvised, deliberately unplanned, and they thereby present a freshness, a spontaneity and an intensity of vision which a more ordered approach might have destroyed. Verve and zest replace solemnity and pretentiousness, for 'un peu d'extravagance sied mieux que de la pédanterie' (*VR* 113). He himself excellently defines his formula:

... ce n'est pas un *Guide* que nous avons la prétention d'écrire; nous voulons seulement peindre, en quelques chapitres familiers, la vie ... d'un voyageur sans parti pris, curieux de tout, très flâneur ... prenant le hasard pour cicerone, et ne parlant ... que de ce qu'il a vu. Ce sont des croquis faits d'après nature, des plaques de daguerréotype, de petits morceaux de mosaïque recueillis sur place, que nous juxtaposons sans trop nous soucier d'une correction et d'une régularité qu'il n'est peut-être pas possible d'obtenir dans une chose aussi diffuse que le vagabond-age à pied ou en gondole d'un feuilletoniste en vacance dans une ville inconnue pour lui, et où tant d'objets tirent la curiosité de tous côtés (*VI* 273).

Gautier combines all the qualities of the great travel writer. If authenticity and fidelity are required, every page reveals his astonishing eye for meticulous detail, re-creating scene, building, people and landscape in striking relief. But it is his insatiable curiosity, his appetite for novel experience, that is perhaps the poet's most valuable asset and which tempers and enlivens his narrative. Arriving fresh 'du fond de notre froide Europe' (*C* 125), Gautier is beside himself with childlike curiosity, 'le principal mobile de la vie' (*VE* 261); and it is this motivating force—and not intellectual enquiry, which he possessed in only average degree—which enables him to surmount the intense physical fatigue of the vast Russian distances, covered in appalling conditions, and generally to confront climatic hazards—which would have daunted most travellers (cf. *VE* 157, *C* 77).

The good-humoured tone and fluency of style contribute greatly to Gautier's success as a travel writer; as Proust remarked, 'chaque phrase . . . accentue et poursuit le trait plein de grâce et de gaieté de sa personnalité'.[8] The embittered Parisian journalist is rejuvenated by the therapy of travel, with its thrill of discovery, and the constant hyperbole is much more than a mere stylistic device. 'Ecrasé de magnificences', 'soûls de chefs-d'œuvre' (*VE* 330, 51) after days of 'éblouissement intellectuel' (*C* 99), the verve and variety of the poetic style reflect the generosity of the author's character.

Gautier's travel writings combine, therefore, lucid, objective reporting with an endearing personal focus which ultimately enhances, rather than detracts from their value as literature. His conscientiousness and integrity never allow him consciously to deform his account, and indeed enable him to furnish a valuable historical record of scene and manners. But this factual reporting is rarely neutral, never clinical; it is heightened and enlivened by an exuberant personality reflected above all in an astonishing verbal facility which makes his work immensely readable.

CRITICISM

To this day one remains astonished at the immense volume of Gautier's critical work, the product of almost forty years of continuous writing on art, literature and the theatre, and also, periodically, on music, ballet, sculpture, architecture and the 'minor' arts. Adolphe Boschot has calculated[9] that in one year alone selected at random (1855), Gautier wrote on average one article every other day, thereby accumulating by his death the equivalent on the Fine Arts alone of about twenty solid volumes. It is, therefore, not surprising that no general study of Gautier's criticism has yet been attempted.[10] Any detailed assessment of such a prodigious output is quite beyond the scope of the present purpose, which is to consider briefly some of the underlying principles of Gautier's approach. Thus our discussion will confine itself to critical writing in two fields only, painting and literature; but it must be stressed that examination of his music and dramatic criticism also would be required before any serious appraisal of the subject could be arrived at.

Art Criticism

In spite of the sheer volume of Gautier's art criticism, he is no longer considered the oracular 'critique incomparable et indispensable'[11] that Baudelaire and others saw in him in the days when artists, writers and even musicians solicited his approbation and were grateful for a sympathetic notice.[12] Recent studies of French art criticism seem unanimously to have decided to omit Gautier from serious consideration.[13] Today his reputation as art critic is completely eclipsed by that of his great contemporary, Baudelaire.

The immediate reasons for this virtually total neglect are in a purely practical sense clear enough. It seems axiomatic that the sheer quantity of Gautier's criticism, much of it hastily improvised, is incompatible with uniform quality; there is indeed much inequality in value, and the good has been submerged with the indifferent. Above all, the fact that much of the critical work appeared in reviews, some ephemeral, and was never published in book form, and that even the fraction that did so appear has not been reprinted since, means that the vast majority of the articles are not easily accessible. No comprehensive selection from this criticism has ever been published. Finally, Gautier's criticism has suffered from the steep decline in the writer's reputation generally.

The impartial student will suspect that such neglect is in some measure unjustified if intrinsic merit is the sole criterion. Comparison with Baudelaire, whose reputation as a critic has soared to new, perhaps exaggerated heights, is unavoidable, but does little to solve the puzzle, since the two poets held similar views on art and Gautier, being the elder of the two, did in fact anticipate Baudelaire's judgement in a number of important specific instances.[14] Leaving aside this comparative issue however, the crucial question which must be posed is clearly: what claims does Gautier possess to be regarded as a major art critic?

Not even Gautier's detractors would deny him several of the most essential qualifications. First, his extraordinary, single-minded passion for the arts, his unshakeable conviction that art was a vital component of everyday life (witness his interest in fashion, in urban planning, the design of domestic china or of locomotives)[15] ensure sympathetic consideration of any work of art. His often criticised leniency to minor artists (Baudelaire once tartly commented that 'M. Théophile Gautier . . . a loué tout le monde')[16] derives from a combination of factors: faulty methods of note-taking, sheer boredom, innate good nature, but above all from the fact that he is over-respectful of any artistic act of faith in face of an alien society.

At the very outset of his career as critic he pronounced his aims: 'Notre critique différera de celle des autres journaux . . en ce que, loin de s'étendre longuement sur les défauts . . . elle s'attachera plutôt à faire ressortir les beautés.'[17] He interpreted his rôle as critic as being primarily one of encouragement of the individual artist, and became conscious that a severe notice from his semi-official pen could easily prejudice an aspiring artist's reputation: 'Si j'avais condamné trop péremptoirement une œuvre d'art . . . j'aurais entravé la carrière de l'artiste et lui aurais souvent volé son pain' (*EB* 164).

Gautier's complete disinterestedness, particularly in the early, independent phase, meant his bold championing of many of the *refusés* in the *Salons* (Corot, Delacroix, Rousseau etc.) and his condemnation of the traditionally-minded selection committees. Touchingly, Gautier's last and unfulfilled ambition as critic was to plan a series of articles entitled 'Ceux qui seront célèbres' in which he would support young, unknown artists (*EB* 210). He possessed, as Banville rightly stressed, the unfashionable 'faculté d'admirer' (*EB* 234).

That he was a rare connoisseur with an unparalleled artistic culture will also be conceded. Baudelaire's homage is significant: 'Théophile Gautier seul peut me comprendre quand je parle peinture'.[18] His cosmopolitanism, again justly stressed by Baudelaire, ensures immense breadth of reference—though he sometimes abuses this by lazily substituting comparison for evaluation. Moreover, his technical knowledge of painting (he was virtually the only French critic of his day with first-hand studio training) and also of the minor arts, although possibly exaggerated, was unequalled among his contemporaries; and this enables him to attempt to assess objectively a talent and a potential even when, as with Monet, Manet, Millet and Courbet, his sympathies are not aroused by their vision. Comments on Théodore Rousseau's brush stroke (*HR* 235) or Goya's engraving techniques (*VE* 115–24) do not, of course, amount to true criticism, although they are part of it; but they do convey an ability to explore an aspect neglected by contemporary criticism, a willingness to evaluate impartially and to seek out the individuality of expression of each artist.

A major virtue of Gautier as critic is his catholicism of taste. Within the elastic limits imposed by his sole criterion—that art must repudiate 'realism' (though not reality) and tend to the ideal—he is undoctrinaire in approach. In an age of artistic dogmatism, polarised in the perennial war between the academic traditionalists and the *refusés*, Gautier is refreshingly free of preconceptions; this was part of Baudelaire's meaning in writing of Gautier's *Salons* that they were oracles 'si calmes, si pleins de candeur et de majesté'.[19] His approach was indeed, by the standards of the day, progressive: 'Nous avons . . . toujours tâché, dans notre critique, de nous mettre au point de vue de l'artiste'; and again: 'Nous admettons chacun au point de vue de son idéal particulier . . . nous épousons momentanément les goûts et les antipathies [des] natures opposées'.[20]

Thus to his credit Gautier avoided the usual sterile disputes between the advocates of line and those of colour[21] and generally adopts a more positive, constructive approach. He could champion, in spite of his love for the classical, the modernity of Gavarni (bracketing him in a major essay with Daumier, Raffet and Doré),[22] praise both Ingres and Delacroix as early as 1832,[23] love Rembrandt and Raphael, Teniers and Tiepolo, Correggio and Michelangelo with equal fervour. Moreover, although Gautier remains attracted to the dramatic or poetic subject, he believes fundamentally that subject is irrelevant[24] and can consequently examine the French landscape school led by Corot and Théodore Rousseau (attacked by Baudelaire in his *Salon de 1859* as 'un genre inférieur . . . culte niais'), English portraitists or Delacroix's historical canvases with equal sympathy. Unlike Baudelaire, Gautier is not worried if the painting in question has no moral overtones.

Naturally Gautier is influenced in his judgements by his personal aesthetics, and this tends to make some of his reactions too predictable. Minor painters like Aligny are praised for their idealism or charm and elevated to the level of Corot (cf. 'A trois Paysagistes', *PN*), major ones like Hogarth or Courbet are dismissed, after some hesitation, on such grounds as didacticism or realism. Again, his myopic, fastidious eye led him to place undue importance on detail and so to overpraise Meissonier. These are of course major deficiencies, as they enable Gautier to sidestep any real appraisal of these artists. Yet this interaction between evaluation of others and formulation of his own aesthetic is endlessly instructive and fascinating.

It is doubtless his antipathy to the Realist School that constitutes Gautier's single greatest failure of imaginative sympathy, prejudicing his assessment of a crucial contemporary trend.[25] Initially he acclaimed both Millet and Courbet (in 1847 and 1849), but later withdrew his praise, considering, along with the general opinion of the day, that realism had been taken too far. Similarly, his veneration for careful composition inevitably renders the Impressionists disagreeable to him. But it must be remembered that the Impressionists were a target of universal hostility (even Baudelaire had grave doubts here), and credit must be given the ageing Gautier for genuinely attempting to appreciate Manet.

Ultimately, however, it is his weakness in interpretive ability which disqualifies Gautier as great art critic. He has the sensitivity to experience a profound emotional impact from a canvas, and also the verbal mastery to communicate this emotion. But he so often lacks the capacity to 'transformer la volupté en connaissance', in Baudelaire's pertinent phrase (*BOC* 1215). He lacks the highest degree of critical intelligence, insight or empathy, which can probe the inner mysteries of a work. Consequently his notices are often allusive commentaries or impressions, tantalisingly undeveloped, rather than true evaluations. His judgement can be erratic and generally lacks the bite and truth of the incisive and subtle Baudelaire.

It is directly due to this imaginative deficiency that he evolved his personal method of descriptive or impressionistic, rather than interpretive criticism, a method basically similar to the poetic transposition. This is not, as Delacroix himself was the first to perceive, criticism in the true sense: 'Il prend un tableau, le décrit à sa manière, fait lui-même un tableau qui est charmant, mais il n'a pas fait acte de véritable critique'.[26] But this technique is both less simple and less sterile than it appears. Sainte-Beuve succinctly defined its true character:

Chaque peinture, chaque fresque, on croit la voir à la lumière dont il la décrit, et on la voit non seulement dans son projet et sa disposition, mais dans son effet et son ton ou sa ligne.[27]

And as Baudelaire pointed out in his *Salon de 1846*, 'le meilleur compte rendu d'un tableau pourra être un sonnet ou une élégie' (*BOC* 877). Also, as we have seen, Gautier conceived of the critic's purpose as essentially a positive, instructive one—hence his popularising works like the *Guide de l'Amateur au Musée du Louvre* and *Les Beaux-Arts en Europe*. Gautier writes in effect, as Baudelaire noted, 'pour tous les exilés qui ne peuvent juger et sentir par leurs propres yeux' (*BOC* 677), and Baudelaire and Sainte-Beuve were convinced of his importance in this purely educative capacity. His purpose as critic merges here with that of the travel writer: to inform, instruct and delight, rather than to evaluate.

Gautier's brand of enlightened superficiality, due in part to his conception of his rôle as critic and in part to innate intellectual deficiency, must exclude him therefore, despite the attractiveness of his writing, from the front rank of art critics who illuminate by profound analysis. Although it is true, as Jules Laforgue asserted, that Gautier was 'le seul salonnier qui ait pris et tenu le public',[28] Baudelaire's own excellent criterion for criticism reveals Gautier's inadequacy clearly. Gautier's criticism is certainly 'amusante et poétique . . . partiale, passionnée', as required by Baudelaire, but ultimately fails because it does not provide a focus 'qui ouvre le plus d'horizons' (*BOC* 877).

It is however quite unjust to dismiss him. Apart from frequent successes of perception amounting to real insight, for example his studies of Correggio, Ingres and Delacroix, Gautier's place as a major critic, 'sagace autant que bienveillant' (*NL* 325), is assured by his courageous support of generations of *refusés*. The generally progressive, modernist nature of his early criticism in particular is noteworthy. He was justly proud, at the end of his life, of having made his début as critic by an enthusiastic notice of Delacroix (cf. *EB* 209). He acclaimed the genius of Corot and

Théodore Rousseau when they were virtually unknown, discovered and championed Doré and the consistently rejected Puvis de Chavannes (both ignored by Baudelaire), and introduced to a parochial public the equally unknown El Greco, Goya and the English School. He confirmed a deepening contemporary appreciation of the Dutch and French eighteenth century schools, and above all proclaimed his admiration for Ingres and Delacroix whose stature he had immediately and consistently recognised. Others could follow where he had shown the way.

Literary Criticism

As a literary critic Gautier is a less controversial, though still relatively unknown figure. A distinction may first be made between his intrinsic merit and his purely influential capacity as literary critic. Thus a work like his early *Les Grotesques* was clearly more important historically than intrinsically. Following Hugo's defence of the 'grotesque' principle in the 'Préface' to *Cromwell*, the essays of *Les Grotesques* reaffirmed the romantic cult of the wry and bizarre, besides contributing greatly to the revival of interest in French writers of the pre-classical period and, particularly, in Villon, to whom Gautier alone among romantic writers drew attention. This work makes no claim to profundity or to original scholarship, though it throws valuable light on Gautier's own aesthetic principles. Nevertheless, in the best of his literary criticism such a distinction becomes meaningless. Thus his Baudelaire article of 1868 is a capital essay from several points of view. Intrinsically valuable in pinpointing many major areas of Baudelaire's genius, it also offers insight into Gautier's own doctrines and sympathies. Above all perhaps, this essay provides an indication of Gautier's influence as critic, for however controversial the exact nature of his evaluation, this single text was almost entirely responsible for Baudelaire's reputation as the father-founder of French decadence, besides contributing greatly, through its enthusiastic reference to Edgar Allan Poe, to the establishment of Poe as a major literary influence in France.

Gautier's literary criticism reflects the same strengths and weaknesses as his art criticism. Generous and undoctrinaire ('il ne fait appel à aucune esthétique, à aucune théorie; il laisse de côté toute idée préconçue . . .', comments Maxime du Camp: op. cit., p. 68), Gautier always attempts to view his subject sympathetically. Although his clear preference is for poetry rather than prose, he devotes a stimulating and penetrating essay, modestly purporting to be no more than a biographical sketch, to Balzac (reprinted in *Souvenirs Romantiques*).

In many of the individual essays, criticism proper is interspersed as usual with lively asides and personal reminiscences which, although strictly irrelevant and potentially exasperating, often have documentary value. This nonchalant technique reaches perfection in his nostalgic records, rhapsodic and evocative rather than critical, of the early romantic battles; indeed his exuberant re-creation of the first night of *Hernani* and his profiles of the various eccentrics of the Petit Cénacle (incorporated in the *Histoire du Romantisme*) are still quoted whenever the atmosphere of the period is evoked.

The method is still, therefore, largely discursive, seemingly improvised, impressionistic; but lacking a visual subject, the descriptive technique of his art criticism often gives way to a lyrical, decorative style which, once Gautier's critical sympathies are engaged, pinpoints a writer's uniqueness and crystallises his genius in imaginative and accomplished prose poems. Perfect examples are furnished by the analyses of Banville's *Les Stalactites* and Baudelaire's Parisian inspiration in *Histoire du Romantisme* (*HR* 301–2, 349) or the extended image of the garden by which he illustrates the genius of Heine (*SR* 258–9). Alternatively, he may linger over some individual poem that he considers of crucial importance to an appreciation of the poet's work: Baudelaire's 'Rêve Parisien' (*HR* 350), Hugo's 'Eviradnus' or 'Le Satyre' (*HR* 392, 395), Vigny's 'Eloa' (*HR* 163), Leconte de Lisle's 'Hypatie' (*HR* 331). Often he can encapsulate a writer's distinctive essence in either a plastic symbol, like that of Vigny's swan (*HR* 164–5), or in a few memorable phrases which go unerringly to the heart of a writer's uniqueness.

It is notoriously difficult to detect and analyse the true originality of one's contemporaries; yet Gautier's appraisals, generous but lucid, almost infallibly single out those major aspects of his subject's genius which posterity has since ratified: Lamartine's idealism and ethereality, Nerval's mysticism, the visionary, apocalyptic inspiration of Hugo. Frequently Gautier's judgement is so perceptive as to be almost prophetic. It was Gautier, for example, who first stressed Lamartine's musicality; Gautier (and not Baudelaire, as has been claimed) who first recognised in Balzac the quality of the visionary ('son grand œil buvait les cieux', 'Balzac fut un *voyant*')[29]—a major contribution to the subsequent appreciation of the novelist. Again, as early as 1852,[30] Gautier recognised Hugo not only as a visionary but as a graphic artist, a judgement not accepted and seriously examined until this century.

If Gautier's value as a critic is generally unacknowledged today, after being considered in his lifetime as 'le premier des critiques contemporains',[31] this is evidently due to a combination of factors: partly to the innate deficiencies we have recognised, but partly also to an evolution in the concept of criticism itself. Judged by Oscar Wilde's standpoint—which coincides with Gautier's own—that 'the critic is he who can translate into another manner or a new material his impression of beautiful things' ('Preface', *Dorian Gray*), Gautier must indeed be counted a major critic. But the modern view is more exacting than this, demanding the sophisticated evaluation that Gautier was often reluctant to attempt. As an interpreter he has evident limitations; yet it must be stressed that his impressionistic appreciations, besides often brilliantly rendering the work under discussion, also frequently imply evaluation and provoke creative thought. The analyses of Hugo, Balzac, Nerval, Heine and Baudelaire are major critical essays by any standards. Above all, Gautier's critical integrity is praiseworthy. His obstinate refusal to extenuate his praise of Hugo under the Second Empire, which nearly cost him his livelihood, is well known.[32] His advice to Bergerat well conveys this integrity:

Regarde avec respect une peinture réputée insensée; écoute jusqu'au bout la musique sifflée . . . Tout le secret de ce qu'on a appelé mon génie critique est là, et je te donne ce conseil pour l'avenir: lis tout, écoute tout et retiens tout . . . Artiste, parle toujours selon ta conscience . . . de l'art (*EB* 157).

FICTION

Gautier's novels and short stories constitute yet another major area of his immense literary output, ranging in extent from brief *contes* like the half-dozen exquisite pages of 'La Nuit des Rossignols' to the 500 dense pages of *Le Capitaine Fracasse*. Gautier had the misfortune to write in a century which saw the greatest competitive expansion of the novel in the history of French literature. Nevertheless, his contribution has not been totally eclipsed by the monumental achievements of his great contemporaries, and *Mademoiselle de Maupin* and *Le Capitaine Fracasse* have even ensured him a still perceptible niche in popular culture.

Short Stories

These are numerous, and fall into three main genres. A first group comprises reminiscences of literary life and includes the series of six tales collected as *Les Jeunes-France* and the two strictly autobiographical narratives describing experiences with drugs, 'La Pipe d'Opium' and 'Le Club des Haschischins'. These accounts are not strictly fiction so much as fictionalised memoires. *Les Jeunes-France*, for example, caricatures from first-hand experience certain prevailing fashionable excesses through a gallery of ultra-romantic portraits, warning against various forms of romantic lunacy. These tales present a triple interest: in their zany and irreverent humour; as an invaluable period document of fashionable manners (particularly spectacular in the vivid hallucinations of 'Le Club des Haschischins'); and for the light they shed on Gautier's personal obsessions. The fantasies of each, rooted in precise reality and then pushed to absurdity, are transparently autobiographical, being used to conjure the author's own apprehensions.

A second subdivision of the short stories corresponds to the genre defined by Baudelaire as Gautier's 'nouvelle poétique' (*BOC* 691), being romances composed to an unrepentently make-believe formula. Often based on amorous quest and intrigue, these combine conventional rather than realistic psychology, colourfully picturesque non-contemporary settings, and a fanciful, extravagant narrative stoutly opposed to the realistic. Most escape from what Gautier contemptuously dismissed as 'la littérature de commissaire-priseur où nous vivons'[33] to a variety of splendidly exotic milieux: the Madrid of bullfights and desperadoes ('Militona'), an Arabian Nights Cairo ('La Mille et Deuxième Nuit'), the paganism of ancient Athens or Egypt ('La Chaîne d'Or', 'Le Roi Candaule', 'Une Nuit de Cléopâtre'), a dreamy, willow-pattern China ('Le Pavillon sur l'Eau'). This frequent removal to a fastidiously and lovingly reconstructed past is both characteristic of the genre and of the author's own incorrigible cult of the *ailleurs*. Two ages were, in their pagan hedonism, particularly irresistible to Gautier: the 'joyeux 18e siècle . . ., l'époque des Ris, des Jeux et des Plaisirs',[34] evoking the world of Marivaux, Rameau and Boucher in the charming rococo frivolities of 'Jean et Jeannette' and 'Le Petit Chien de la Marquise'; and the aura of barbaric grandeur and idealism of the pre-Christian era ('Une Nuit de Cléopâtre', 'La Chaîne d'Or', 'Le Roi Candaule'). These latter tales anticipate the more extended *Le Roman de la Momie* in their spectacular documentation.[35] Somewhat different, however, are those romances whose dream atmosphere, naivety and inconsequentiality give them the character of romantic fairy-tales: 'La Mille et Deuxième Nuit', 'L'Ame de la Maison', and, above all, the elegant poignancy of 'Le Pavillon sur l'Eau', 'Le Nid des Rossignols,' and 'L'Enfant aux Souliers de Pain'. These haunting tales are, regrettably, a virtually unknown part of Gautier's production.

Perhaps the best-known of Gautier's short stories is the third group, the series of *contes fantastiques* in which the supernatural, already introduced incidentally in the two previous genres, becomes the dominant and obtrusive factor, motivating the intrigue and assuming a deliberately unnerving character. Describing himself as 'un conteur fantastique',[36] Gautier explores the world of the occult, adopting the Hoffmannesque formula of confronting the supernatural with everyday reality and indeed employing many of Hoffmann's recurrent devices: animation of the inanimate, doppelgänger and schizoid effects, hallucinations, macabre nocturnal happenings. As was noted in considering 'Albertus', to Gautier's early cult of Hoffmann[37] and the general romantic addiction to the supernatural must be added the poet's intimacy with Nerval, Balzac and Esquiros, all devotees of the occult, and his own incorrigibly superstitious nature.[38]

These stories are based on the underlying assumption that consciousness exists simultaneously on several planes, spatially and temporally. Distance and time cease to have meaning, and, in particular, normal, everyday consciousness hides a more mysterious, elusive reality to which access is allowed through various means: drugs,[39] dreams, and various states of mental hyperactivity. Subtle relationships bind us to other worlds. Love especially allows communion between souls through space and time, and a recurrent leitmotiv is the Nervalian quest for a lost love materialised in a feminine ideal glimpsed either retrospectively ('Omphale', 'La Cafetière', 'Arria Marcella', *Le Roman de la Momie*) or in the future (*Spirite*).

This quest, or attempt to repossess a lost ideal, in itself poignantly autobiographical, is pursued with an intensity that deranges the mind and forces alienation from life. But detachment from materiality is a first prerequisite of happiness: 'Le monde réel n'existait plus pour moi, et tous les liens qui m'y attachaient étaient rompus: mon âme, dégagée de sa prison de boue, nageait dans le vague et l'infini'.[40] In some stories the hero attains his ideal, but only momentarily, in a dream state, before reawakening to sordid reality; most are therefore stories of failures. Malivert alone, in *Spirite*, attains felicity, through physical dissolution.

These fantasies keep intact, beyond the Hoffmannesque twists of reality, a sense of pervading mystery and idealism which, influenced by the revelation of the second *Faust*,[41] reaches a climax in the mysticism of 'Arria Marcella' and, above all, in the Platonic myth *Spirite*, conveying Gautier's unrequited passion for Carlotta Grisi in magnificent lyrical passages expressing the soul's yearning for its definitive liberation.[42]

Novels

Mademoiselle de Maupin

Written intermittently during 1833–5, *Mademoiselle de Maupin* appeared in two volumes in 1835 and 1836. Together with its celebrated polemical 'Préface' of 1834, this 'artistic bible of a whole generation'[43] constitutes a major document of the times. Widely acclaimed but 'plus célèbre que connue' (*AR* 283), the novel has always provoked the most diverse reactions (see below, pp. 117–18). In general, writers, beginning with Hugo and Balzac, enthused over its magnificent style and, like Baudelaire and Swinburne, acclaimed its aestheticism, the latter defining it as 'the holy writ of beauty'.[44] On the other hand its supposedly scabrous subject of bisexual relationships (its subtitle was *Double Amour*) ensured it a *succès de scandale* typified by Mirecourt's stress on the satanic, potentially corrupting element of 'cette œuvre sans nom',[45] and this endeared it to the decadent movement.

Although loosely based on scandalous episodes in the life of a mysterious seventeenth century heroine in whom interest had recently been revived,[46] the novel is, like all Gautier's fiction, strongly autobiographical. The somewhat tortuously structured action ('plus entortillé et plus compliqué qu'un imbroglio espagnol' laughs the author: *MM* 86), though relatively unimportant in itself, should not be dismissed, as some commentators have done, as 'an apologia of Lesbian love',[47] as merely 'a wildly emotional fantasy about sex'.[48] The fiction clothes, in fact, an important, if unoriginal, metaphysical statement of human dissatisfaction. Like the almost contemporary 'Fortunio', the novel is a pagan 'hymne à la beauté, à la richesse, au bonheur' ('Préface', 'Fortunio'), and this cult is identified with love, a love independent of distinction of sex and therefore of any restrictive morality. This concept is provocatively illustrated in the hermaphrodite theme which, though fashionable at the time and given new topicality by the ambiguous relationship between the actress Marie Dorval and George Sand,[49] fuses two major preoccupations of Gautier: the idealist yearning for the unattainable (Gautier's lovers are, like Baudelaire's lesbians, 'chercheurs d'infini'), and the harmonious combination of opposites.

Once the true nature of *Mademoiselle de Maupin* is appreciated its so-called defects as an orthodox novel—disunity, incoherent characterisation, anachronism—become irrelevant. Ultimately, it is precisely in the 'digressions' that the interest and value of the work reside. The period charm, the indeterminate local colour, the surface eroticism all pale beside the burning and poignant analysis of youthful idealism, conveyed with astonishing stylistic virtuosity. For Gautier's youthful prose is already varied and assured, encompassing the analytical, as in the searching psychological debates, the descriptive, as in the enchanting interludes like the nightingale idyll in the moonlit garden (*MM* 130–2), and the rhapsodic, as above all in the many fervent hymns to beauty.

Le Capitaine Fracasse

Promised to the public as early as 1836, but continually postponed, *Le Capitaine Fracasse* finally appeared in book form in November 1863. It immediately achieved a popularity which it has maintained almost undiminished to the present day, besides earning for the impecunious author a welcome state pension. Beloved, amongst many others, of Baudelaire, Verlaine and Proust,[50] the novel represents the fulfilment of a youthful project, a 'vieux rêve presque oublié', to write a novel around the character of Fracasse, the stock soldier of the traditional Italian comedy.

The novel belongs therefore essentially, as Gautier himself declares in his 'Avant-Propos', to the flamboyant 1830s, turning its back resolutely and provocatively on the very different spirit of the 1860s: 'Nous nous sommes autant que possible séparé du milieu actuel, et nous avons vécu rétrospectivement, nous reportant vers 1830, aux beaux jours du romantisme'. In consequence *Fracasse* fuses the fervour and idealism of the period of *Mademoiselle de Maupin* with those qualities—panache, chivalry, a roguish sense of adventure—which the nostalgic poet associates with his favourite period, that of Louis XIII, which is the novel's historical setting. It is therefore, in a double sense, a 'roman rétrospectif'.[51]

Furthermore, Gautier as author of *Les Grotesques* specifically associates his hero with Scarron's *Roman Comique*, and in the 'Avant-Propos' invites the reader to view his novel as a transposition of a series of engravings by the seventeenth century Callot and Abraham Bosse—an analogy further pointed by the strong seventeenth century flavour of the engravings of Gautier's friend Gustave Doré for the 1866 edition of the novel.

This time, the picaresque action of the novel is relatively straightforward, and crystallises around a series of unforgettable set-piece tableaux which are astonishingly vivid *tours de force*: the opening description of the dilapidated castle ('Le Château de la Misère'), the snow scene ('Effet de Neige'), the sordid Parisian tavern ('Le Radis Couronné'). Once again in Gautier's work the parts are of greater value than the whole, and ideology is more than ever sacrificed to extravagant colour:

On n'y trouvera aucune thèse politique, morale ou religieuse. Nul grand problème ne s'y débat. On n'y plaide pour personne. L'auteur n'y exprime jamais son opinion. C'est une œuvre purement pittoresque. ('Avant-Propos')

Gone too, at last, is the personal anguish always present in the *contes* and in *Mademoiselle de Maupin*. Or almost: for, as Gautier admitted, certain episodes transpose his own dejection[52] and, in a sense, the wandering actors enact a poignant masquerade on the tragi-comic destiny of man:

Un chariot comique contient tout un monde. En effet, le théâtre n'est-il pas la vie en raccourci, le véritable microcosme . . . ne renferme-t-il pas dans son cercle l'ensemble des choses et des diverses fortunes humaines? (ch. v)

But the overriding impression which remains is of a bravura fantasy. As Sainte-Beuve noted, a certain tonal note is struck at the outset to which, in spite of its episodic nature, the entire novel remains consistent: 'Cela lui imposait tout un langage et un style continu, une sorte de gamme et d'échelle harmonique où, la clef une fois donnée, rien ne fît fausse note et ne détonnât'.[53] The novel acquires thereby a unity often lacking in Gautier's work, and a seductive, juvenile allure which finds its perfect expression in the pastiche of the effervescent, pre-Malherbian *précieux* style which Gautier claimed as a lost artistic ideal.[54] For almost the last time, in the sparkle and enchantment of this cloak-and-dagger fairy tale in which all live happily ever after, the ageing poet momentarily recaptures his youthful ardour to linger in his native Gascony and fill it with his dreams.

V

GAUTIER'S FORTUNE AND INFLUENCE

IN FRANCE

Gautier was slow in winning acclaim; indeed, his importance as a poet has only ever been recognised by a minority, a fact which perplexed Sainte-Beuve from the outset: 'Je me demande . . . pourquoi . . . le succès de Gautier s'est longtemps confiné et se renferme encore dans un cercle d'artistes et de connaisseurs'.[1] That the early poetry achieved only limited success was due to a combination of factors: the unfortunate coincidence of the 1830 Revolution, the insufficiently distinctive character of the poetry itself, and the more spectacular achievements of Gautier's gifted elders Lamartine, Vigny and Hugo. *Le Figaro*'s verdict was typical of the general reaction: 'sa poésie est toute couleur et nulle d'idées'.[2] In short, Gautier's early poems made little impact; they provoked, as Houssaye later remarked of *Les Jeunes-France*, 'du bruit dans le monde littéraire mais ne pénétrèrent pas beaucoup dans le monde qui lit'.[3]

It was the series of articles later to become *Les Grotesques*, and the controversy they aroused, which first brought Gautier's name before the public. With the subsequent 'Préface' to *Mademoiselle de Maupin* the young author suddenly appears to assert his individuality and become an influential figure, challenging widely accepted notions. The *succès de scandale* of the novel itself, following the turbulent episode of *Hernani* and the pink waistcoat, contributed further to create a mildly disreputable prestige.

However, Gautier's stand was important on purely literary terms too. The provocative aestheticism and the pagan ideal celebrated in *Mademoiselle de Maupin* diverged sharply from the social and moral direction much romantic literature was taking at the time, as Gautier himself later recalled with some pride: 'ç'a été une scission, quand j'ai chanté l'antiquité . . . j'ai fait faire une bifurcation à l'école du romantisme'.[4] The whole subsequent aesthetic movement of the century is indebted to the impetus given to decadent hedonism by *Mademoiselle de Maupin*.

Compared at once to the *Mémoires* of the criminal Lacenaire and the writings of de Sade, the novel acquired a taint of satanism, decadence and obscenity which remained with it well into the twentieth century.

Gautier's professional début as a regular journalist in 1836, directly due to Balzac's enthusiasm for *Mademoiselle de Maupin*,[5] marked an important new stage in his literary fortune and, as he acknowledged,[6] earned him an even wider reputation. His reviews, particularly of the *Salons* where he could be caustic as well as generous, soon established his reputation as one of the major critics of the day; and this position was consolidated by his dramatic criticism for *La Presse* and, later, by his founding the influential *Revue de Paris* in 1851 and co-directing *L'Artiste* from 1857. One of his major achievements as critic was his revelation of Wagner to the French as early as 1857, while touching letters reached him asking his critical blessing on unknown composers.[7]

It was through the dual nature of his literary presence—as critic and theorist on the one hand, as imaginative writer on the other—that Gautier gradually acquired an unrivalled prestige in cultural circles. It is difficult to exaggerate his importance as a key figure in the intellectual landscape of mid-century France. With the disappearance of the great romantics, Gautier now remained the sole authoritative voice of romantic idealism. Moreover, his hellenism, his acknowledged connoisseurship, his intransigent hostility to so-called bourgeois values and, above all, the character of his own work with its qualities of precision, colour, line and apparent objectivity made him the focal point of that interpenetration of the plastic and literary arts so characteristic of the times. He himself pinpointed his vital contribution in his statement of editorial policy in *L'Artiste* of 14 December 1856:

Nous donnerons à l'art proprement dit une place plus large qu'à la littérature ... nous ferons asseoir la poésie dans un musée ... Après avoir vu, notre plus grand plaisir a été de transporter dans notre art à nous monuments, fresques, tableaux, statues, bas-reliefs, au risque souvent de forcer la langue et de changer le dictionnaire en palette.

One specific illustration of Gautier's impact in mid-century is provided by the case of the octosyllabic quatrain. Speaking modestly of *Emaux et Camées*, Gautier writes of the octosyllable: 'Cette forme . . . fut accueillie assez favorablement, et les vers de huit pieds groupés en quatrains devinrent pour quelque temps un sujet d'exercice parmi les jeunes poètes' (*HR* 323)—a claim amply borne out by the verse of Banville, Coppée, Heredia, Sully Prudhomme and others.

Exerting an influence at once diffuse and clearly definable therefore, Gautier became the acknowledged 'Maître du Parnasse',[8] opposing pagan qualities of harmony and perfection to the restlessness and degeneracy of contemporary life and thereby influencing the head of the Parnassian school, Leconte de Lisle.[9] The works of many of the major writers of the period bear eloquent testimony to the debts they owed Gautier. In spite of periodic reservations on Gautier's talent, Baudelaire, for example, besides marvelling at his virtuosity and seeing him as a bulwark against contemporary fatuity, gleaned much from Gautier. Undeniable and impressive evidence of large numbers of direct borrowings from Gautier has been amassed in numerous specialised studies of the relationship between the two poets.[10]

Both Balzac and Flaubert revered Gautier for the same qualities of craftsmanship, colour and pugnacity. Balzac frequently collaborated with Gautier and was not above plagiarising him on occasion,[11] while Flaubert 'ne jurait que par lui; il accueillait sans les discuter toutes [ses] idées'.[12] Maxime du Camp, a familiar of both writers, records Gautier's influence on Flaubert's *Novembre*; *Madame Bovary* was hailed at its appearance as being stylistically indebted to Gautier,[13] while Houssaye's anecdote recording *Le Roman de la Momie* as direct source of *Salammbô* is well known.[14]

Gautier's influence on the late nineteenth century novel generally is indeed a capital one. Faguet went as far as to affirm: 'Gautier a eu une influence décisive sur le roman de 1850 à 1900 . . . Que le roman soit devenu une œuvre d'art . . . c'est exactement à Théophile Gautier que nous le devons . . .'[15] Fromentin's *débuts* were actively fostered by Gautier[16], while the Goncourt brothers in particular (who in 1864 dedicated *Renée Mauperin* to Gautier) shared many of Gautier's profoundest convictions, declaring: 'Nous faisons, à nous trois avec Gautier, le camp retranché de l'art pour l'art, de la moralité du Beau, de l'indifférence en matière politique . . .'[17] It was Gautier's extravagant aestheticism which encouraged and sharpened the Goncourts' remarkable visual acuity and which provoked in them their *écriture artiste*.[18] Similarly, Gautier's influence on Huysmans was equally crucial.[19]

Gautier's incalculable influence on Parnassian poetry and aesthetics on the one hand and on the development of the novel on the other is widely acknowledged. That he should also be a source of symbolism finds less willing acceptance. The undeniable representational element in his work has seemed incompatible with 'pure' poetry and with the fundamentally mystical, transcendental basis of French symbolism. Yet Baudelaire, Rimbaud and Mallarmé—none of whom was given to indiscriminate praise—perceived that Gautier's poetry contained depths unexplored by much orthodox Parnassian poetry. Nor would Hugo himself have applied the significant term *mage* to Gautier ('A Théophile Gautier', *Toute la Lyre*) had he considered Gautier's qualities confined to strictly Parnassian ones.

In a well-known passage Baudelaire praised in Gautier his 'immense intelligence innée de la *correspondance* et du symbolisme universels', conveyed uniquely by 'une espèce de sorcellerie évocatoire' (*BOC* 689–90). Rimbaud likewise, including Gautier later in his privileged élite of *voyants* (Letter to Demeny, 15 May 1871), did not hesitate to incorporate numerous borrowings from Gautier—what he termed his *rinçures*—into his own poetry.[20]

Verlaine too, who it is known possessed many of Gautier's works of which he thought highly and who defended Gautier on several occasions,[21] reveals affinities with Gautier so strong as to suggest direct imitation in specific instances. The elusive, wistful, pre-Verlainian tone in Gautier which we have already noted is significant; and even without the often-quoted parallel between *Fêtes Galantes* and 'Variations sur le Carnaval de Venise', many comparisons offer proof of direct borrowings.[22]

Even more striking is the case of Mallarmé, in whose poetic formation Gautier was, with Banville and Baudelaire, a major influence. Mallarmé admired in Gautier not only 'l'impeccable artiste', one of the 'maîtres inaccessibles dont la beauté me désespère' ('Symphonie Littéraire')—the 'Parnassian' Gautier— but saluted him later as a 'voyant',[23] an 'œil profond' who transmutes nature into quintessential forms ('Toast Funèbre'). Even more than themes (purity, narcissism, depersonalisation, the curious alternation of the chaste and the sensual), specific *précieux* motifs (flowers, mirrors, precious stones, whiteness) and even some key vocabulary ('azur', 'aboli', 'nul') constantly recall Gautier throughout Mallarmé's verse. Gautier's 'Ténèbres' (*CM*) inspired the *terza rime* of 'Le Guignon',[24] the great 'Toast Funèbre' is steeped in precise echoes of Gautier,[25] Gautier's Nyssia in 'Le Roi Candaule' anticipates Hérodiade, as in *Emaux et Camées* Gautier's swan ('Fantaisies d'Hiver') and swan-maiden ('Symphonie en Blanc majeur') inspired Mallarmé's own swan ('Le Vierge, le vivace'). From Gautier's stress on the sacred nature of poetry, his cult of the artificial, his idealism, his *préciosité*, derives much that is most characteristic in Mallarmé's mature work. Gautier's injunction about the necessity of a 'rythme oculaire' in poetry became a key principle in the Mallarmé of the posthumous 'Un Coup de Dés'; while Mallarmé's ideal theatre—and the symbolist theatre in general—is indebted to Gautier's own ideal.[26] Many features common to Gautier and Mallarmé subsequently reappear in Valéry (who greatly admired Gautier, especially in adolescence) and would repay careful examination.[27]

Such testimonies from exceptionally perceptive artists may not easily be dismissed. The fact is that, valuing in Nerval, Balzac and Baudelaire the qualities of the *voyant*,[28] Gautier was receptive to and actively encouraged the 'mystical form of Aestheticism known as symbolism' whose essence, writes C. M. Bowra, 'is its insistence on a world of ideal beauty, and its conviction that this is realised through art'.[29] This had been Gautier's own programme from the start.

On his death tribute was paid to him in the commemorative *Le Tombeau de Théophile Gautier*, published by Lemerre in 1873, which comprised the homage of many writers and which culminated in the two magnificent and moving tributes of Mallarmé and Hugo, 'Toast Funèbre' and 'A Théophile Gautier'. Yet for all the admiration of fellow writers, the public knew Gautier only as a journalist, ironically the aspect of his work he himself discounted. He remained, and tends to remain to this day, essentially a poet's poet. Posthumously, the prevailing climate became increasingly alien to his fundamental poetic temper. By the end of the century, Romanticism, Le Parnasse and Art for Art's Sake seemed, in spite of the work of fervent minorities, already remote, short-lived irrelevances in the dynamic acceleration which thrust Europe forward towards 1914, when Péguy noted that the world had changed less since Jesus Christ than in the last thirty years. In spite of the painstaking efforts of Spoelberch de Lovenjoul, who compiled a detailed record of Gautier's complete works,[30] Gautier's prestige was undermined and he has never recaptured his former eminence. At least in France, Gautier's poetry had seemingly little place.

IN ENGLAND AND THE UNITED STATES

By the late 1850s and early 1860s, Gautier had begun to acquire a reputation in England, and the commemorative *Tombeau* of 1873 included tributes from several English poets. The greatest channel for Gautier's growing prestige in England, and for poetic aestheticism in general, was Swinburne, who considered Gautier 'the most luminous of all poets'[31] and who offered the major English contribution to the *Tombeau*. Swinburne's 'Notes on Poems and Reviews' had in 1866 consciously recalled the Preface to *Mademoiselle de Maupin*, while he acclaimed the novel itself as 'the most perfect and exquisite book of modern times'.[32] Seeing in Gautier's verse 'the faultless and secure expression of an exclusive worship of things formally beautiful',[33] Swinburne included in his *Poems and Ballads* of 1866 actual pastiches of Gautier's poems.[34] Swinburne's initiative 'opened through Victorian reticence the breach which, gradually widened, eventually let in the flood of decadent literature'.[35]

Many others followed Swinburne's lead. Austin Dobson later adapted Gautier's 'L'Art' in his 'Ars Victrix' (1877), while Pater, D. G. Rossetti, John Payne[36] and others continued the same strain of French aestheticism. George Moore went as far as to see Gautier as 'the highest peak of the literary mountain' and to affirm of Gautier's works that 'were I to live for a thousand years, their power on my soul would remain unshaken. I am what they made me'.[37] Through such disciples Gautier was able post-humously to influence the *fin de siècle* climate in England as well as in France. French decadence saw its first English manifesto in Arthur Symons' 'The Decadent Movement in Literature' (1893), heavily based on Gautier's defence of *Les Fleurs du Mal*, and Symons and the Rhymers Club, Whistler and, particularly, Oscar Wilde[38] were all directly indebted to Gautier.

Finally, a vital modern ramification of Gautier's aesthetic formalism crystallised early in this century around the association between Ezra Pound and T. S. Eliot, with their common admiration for Gautier. Henry James had long ago devoted a major essay to Gautier in his *French Poets and Novelists* of 1878 (stressing incidentally that Baudelaire was 'an altogether inferior genius to Gautier') and thus established Gautier's reputation in American university circles.[39] Joining the Imagists in London in April 1909 Pound championed their poetic ideal of 'absolutely accurate presentation and no verbiage'[40] and came to see in Gautier one of the 'poètes essentiels', admired for his 'hardness'.[41]

Eliot for his part noted 'the continuous syntactical variety of Gautier'[42] and used Gautier's octosyllabic quatrain in the poems of 1920. Referring respectfully to Gautier again in the Andrew Marvell essay of 1921, Eliot's Baudelaire essay of 1930 went further in placing Gautier higher than Baudelaire in formal perfection.[43] Both Pound and Eliot united in prescribing *Emaux et Camées* as a remedy against what Pound termed 'the dilution of *vers libre*' and romantic 'swish' and 'swash',[44] and it is not surprising therefore to find frequent echoes of Gautier in Pound and Eliot, both in the form of submerged quotation and in the virtues of compression and plasticism within the close-knit structure of the octosyllabic quatrain. In 'Hugh Selwyn Mauberley' in particular, it has been noted, 'Gautier is the over-riding influence' through which the French poet 'repeatedly enabled Pound to surpass himself'.[45] Via Eliot, Pound and the Imagists the astringency of modern poetry owes much to Gautier's example in combating didacticism, sentimentality and formlessness.

VI

CRITICAL EVALUATION

Retrospectively Gautier appears clearly a pivotal figure not only between the heroical Romanticism and the disillusioned aestheticism of the Parnassian years but between outworn literary conventions and a truly modern viewpoint on art. Gautier's new rôle in this evolution, assumed with a kind of impudent purity, was a major one. After its initial triumphs a critical stage had been reached in the romantic adventure with the questioning of the artist's 'validity' by an influential section of society. Uneasy over the increasing pressures being brought to bear on the artist, Gautier and his disciples perceived that romanticism was in danger of losing itself through its own over-generous spirit in a plethora of ideologies which threatened not only the livelihood but the very integrity of the artist. Gautier thereby became the focal point of what Jasinski terms 'un romantisme rajeuni'[1] in pioneering a deliberately non-seismographic art entirely emancipated from the fashionable concept of artistic relevance, and in pursuing an intellectual, morally neutral form of beauty.

The long-term effect was to legitimise many kinds of socially irresponsible 'pure' poetry, to encourage a self-contained art, 'une poésie née d'elle-même', as Mallarmé approvingly noted of Gautier's own poetry.[2] Such an evolution, of inestimable consequence for the development of modern poetry, operated through the impulsion given by Gautier in certain key areas.

His progressive exclusion of subjects which invite moral judgement shook, if it did not annihilate, the tenacious concept of the hierarchy of genres, the age-old assumption that certain subjects were somehow intrinsically more valid than others. Putting it another way, Gautier decided, in Ezra Pound's simple statement, 'that certain things were worth making into poems'.[3] In practice, Gautier elevated the tradition of occasional verse into what Baudelaire termed 'le dilettantisme en littérature', preaching the Kantian doctrine of disinterested artistic pleasure through the treatment of trivialities. While Hugo and Baudelaire plumb the depths of human anguish, Gautier is composing pieces to an ear-ring, a navel, a scratch, a turnip. Ostentatiously abandoning the romantic ideal of 'total' poetry associated with elevated insight, Gautier moves significantly nearer the concept of the absolute work of art associated with modern formalistic theories.

The corollary is, therefore, the prestige with which Gautier surrounds the concept of style. If content is devalued, questions of form are automatically highlighted, and Gautier played a crucial rôle with Hugo in the issue—of unique importance in French literary history—of the renewal of poetic language, and especially in its evolution from the 'soft' to the 'hard', to use Ezra Pound's terms again. By his contribution to sheer linguistic awareness, his timely rescue of earlier, exuberant patterns of language, and his stress on colour and precision, Gautier acceler-ated the demise of neo-classicism's amorphous rhetoric and contributed incalculably to the creation of a flexible, uninhibited, essentially modern style not only in France but, as we noted in the previous chapter, in English and American poetry too. When to this influence is added his considerable impact on late nineteenth century French prose style, it appears that Banville was largely justified in admiring in Gautier 'le plus robuste artisan de la langue moderne' (*EB* 232). As Sainte-Beuve declared unequivoc-ally of Gautier: 'il a fait rendre à notre langue plus qu'elle ne pouvait jusque-là'.[4]

Equally crucial was the dismissal, by implication, of com-munication theories of art. With Gautier, poetry no longer makes claim to universality, to be accessible to all; the notion of 'the public' becomes largely irrelevant. Poetry is turned not outwards, to 'connect', but inwards, to share with a coterie of connoisseurs an essentially contemplative act involving a wide-ranging, allusive *divertissement*. Such 'private' poetry indeed may go further and treat man only marginally, or not at all. With Gautier the old anthropocentric orientation of literature gives place to all that is non-man—a point stressed by Baudelaire's perceptive note that Gautier 'darde vivement son regard sur le non-moi' (*BOC* 679). Poetry becomes a sort of pure intuition of formal beauty little related to the human substance—a logical tendency in the poet who exclaimed: 'L'homme est laid, partout et toujours, et il me gâte la création' (*EB* 128).

Retrospectively Gautier's achievement appears little short of radical because the repercussions of Art for Art's Sake were so far-reaching. Reviving the view of poetry as art, rather than emotion, he decelerates and depersonalises romanticism, thereby performing a therapy of concentration necessary to its continued development. Baudelaire is quite categorical: '. . . il a même ajouté des forces à la poésie française, . . . il en a agrandi le répertoire et augmenté le dictionnaire . . .' (*BOC* 723-4).

Yet one may perhaps concede Gautier's historical importance but still deny him intrinsic value, adopting Gide's view that 'Gautier occupe une place considérable; c'est seulement fâcheux qu'il la remplisse si mal'.[5] Ultimately such judgements remain subjective; but at least an attempt may be made to establish the main characteristics of Gautier's poetry, relating them to the social and psychological factors in which his art is so clearly rooted.

Although straightforward causal relationships between socio-logical and cultural patterns are seldom easy to determine, the relation of Gautier's art to the immediate external context on the one hand and to temperamental and psychological factors on the other appears clearly substantiated by considerable evidence. It has been suggested that all mannerist art thrives in a climate of sociological alienation and that in particular the specific form of 'Art for Art's Sake' develops when the gulf between the aims of the artist and those of the society to which he belongs appears unbridgeable (cf. above, pp. 18-19). Vis-à-vis the dominant nineteenth century social and political patterns, Gautier's position, expressed pungently in many a legendary diatribe, is an uncompromisingly independent one which inevitably isolates him from society. He represents, in effect, an extreme form of that intellectual malaise in which age-old humanitarian assumptions are challenged and certain disruptive, paranoic elements come to the fore. 'Désireux de la vie et ne pouvant pas vivre' ('Thébaïde', *CM*), Gautier's tragic dilemma is acute, and is exacerbated by the haunting terror of death. Moreover, the disintegration of the individual mirrors the canker in society as a whole, itself prefiguring a wider, cosmic cataclysm. In a 'société qui retombe au chaos' ('Paris', *P*) and in which 'l'univers entier devient paralytique' ('Thébaïde', *CM*), man, displaced from the centre, is relegated to a 'pauvre atome perdu, point dans l'immensité' ('Départ', *E*), and Gautier has a terrifying vision of the imminent abyss: 'Oubli et néant, c'est tout l'homme' (*MM* 209).

Man's saving dignity, the supreme redemption, is his concept of the beautiful. Art is a concerted attack on the given, a refusal to submit to the condition of mortality. Filled with the sense of inadequacy and the neuroticism associated with the 'decadent' mentality, Gautier is led to polarise his views and reappraise the nature and function of art. Living, as he argues, at the extreme verge of civilisation in time, a decadent art is not only appropriate but inevitable: freshness of vision and positive conceptual thinking being ineffectual, the artist must explore the apparent inconsequentialities of individual mannerism. In classing Gautier psychologically as the type of 'esthétique décadent', a recent commentator[6] has merely developed the poet's own admission: 'Nous sommes des malades . . . des décadents . . .'[7] From the outset, Gautier had noted,

Je fus assez bon élève, mais avec des curiosités bizarres qui ne plaisaient pas toujours aux professeurs . . . je me plaisais à imiter les styles qu'au collège on appelle de décadence. J'étais souvent taxé de barbarie . . . (*SR* 5).

Characterising himself as a 'champignon vénéneux' (*MM* 158), Gautier's identification with decadent attitudes is constantly evident: in his admiration for the eccentric 'Grotesques', in the cult of pagan hedonism, in the lure of the artificial, the perverse and the occult, in the championing of artists like Gustave Moreau and Puvis de Chavannes (regulars at his Neuilly dinners), in the search for refined forms of escapism which made 'Fortunio' the model for Huysmans' *A Rebours*.[8] *Mademoiselle de Maupin* alone is a veritable compendium of such themes.

Decadent above all, perhaps, is that neurotic mannerism which provokes, in his analysis of Baudelaire, Gautier's most eloquently revealing definition of 'le style de décadence',

. . . écoutant pour les traduire les confidences subtiles de la névrose, les aveux de la passion vieillissante qui se déprave et les hallucinations bizarres de l'idée fixe tournant à la folie (*SR* 286).

The result is in Gautier an essentially fragmented art, deliberately irresponsible and subversive, crystallising around certain interrelated attitudes which constantly nourish his art: a tendency to introspection leading to narcissim, dandyism and dilettantism on the one hand, the urge to depersonalise and materialise responses in the cult of the artificial on the other.

From all this deep ambiguities result. The lucid artist is under no illusions as to the ultimate viability of his creative act. The fear that not only life but even art itself is an illusory fabric haunts Gautier's work and illuminates his obsession with the themes of metamorphosis, permanence and transience, appearance and reality, as well as specific imagery like that relating to mirrors.[9] Faced with his ideal, the artist experiences 'le sentiment de l'impuissance relative à son art', causing 'l'incurable mélancolie et l'inquiétude sans trêve des grands hommes'.[10] Moreover, any externalisation of a vision necessarily betrays the ideal: 'Les poètes sont ainsi.—Leur plus beau poème est celui qu'ils n'ont pas écrit' (*MM* 168). Hesitantly, Gautier points towards the myth of poetic sterility which was to preoccupy Rimbaud, Mallarmé and Valéry.[11]

A deep irony permeates Gautier's work therefore. Akin to Albertus, in whom 'le bas semblait railler le haut' (*A*, LX), Gautier presents the same curious dichotomy as Byron or Hoffmann, in whom scepticism and mockery are constant correctives of the lyrical, asserting the dignity of man by affirming his self-control. In Gautier the self-parody, the deliberate dissociation, the affectation of impassivity constitute a defence mechanism against deception and vulnerability, a recognition too of the ambivalence of reality. An innate emotionalism is constantly dogged by a lucid, analytical approach, what Banville called Gautier's 'saine ironie'.[12] Gautier embodies strikingly Schiller's formula, derived from Kant, of the unification of the rational and the sensuous in the play instinct. This may be illustrated by considering briefly some of the ways in which Gautier's 'play' operates through individual mannerism, particularly through the visual and verbal imagination which lend his poetry its peculiar character.

The extraordinary visual acuity of the poet, with his 'œil de rat ou de myope',[13] has become legendary: 'toute ma vie, je n'ai fait que m'appliquer à bien voir'.[14] Gautier appears the poet of the immediate and the palpable, respectful of the separateness and self-sufficiency of individual elements of perceived reality, and Mallarmé stressed that this in itself was a rare triumph: 'placé dans le monde, [Gautier] l'a regardé, ce qu'on ne fait pas'.[15]

This achievement should not, however, blur an evident point: that Gautier's perception, concentrated and vivid though it is, is modified by various organisational processes which interfere with any objective transmission of reality. If Gautier sees more constantly and more intensely than other poets, he also sees more selectively. He renders with extraordinary precision certain limited aspects of creation, particularly the isolated and diminutive, but tends to ignore mass, structure and relationship. His favourite poetic techniques include, therefore, enumeration and fragmentation; his idols are the cult of detail, of variety. Moreover, Gautier's vision is usually ordered by a desire to prettify, to idealise or to fantasise—hence the whimsical personification, the stylisation, the plastic symbols or allegories which are far from 'natural'. Paradoxically, therefore, the world which Gautier's vision renders is ultimately one remote from observed reality; he follows Pope's injunction to 'follow Nature . . . but Nature methodised' ('An Essay on Criticism').

The reason is Gautier's concept of art as being essentially decorative. A decoration should charm by excluding austerity and transfiguring reality, and in spite of successful attempts at critical objectivity he ultimately judged artists by their degree of charm, in inverse proportion to their realism: Murillo and Boucher are rated high, Hogarth and Courbet low. After all, 'un beau masque vaut mieux qu'une vilaine face' (*A*, LXXII). Decoration is not mere prettiness, however; the urge towards ornamentation is, as we have seen, proof of man's innate superiority over amorphous nature.

Gautier's eye for the decorative potential of a subject is everywhere apparent, but is particularly striking in solemn subjects where ornamentation risks trivialisation. His fear of death, for example, appears momentarily allayed by its sheer aesthetic appeal. Torn between the sensuous pagan concept of death and the macabre Christian one, Gautier feels an equal aesthetic thrill: the beauty of pyre and urn, the revels of 'amours, ægipans et bacchantes' or the almost Pharaonic cosmetic rites on the one hand (cf. 'Bûchers et Tombeaux', 'Coquetterie Posthume', *EC*); the exquisite chiaroscuro of moonlit cemeteries or the riot of form and colour in gothic vaults on the other ('La Comédie de la Mort'). Physical agony too is exploited aesthetically: carnage ('Le Thermodon', *CM*), martyrdom ('A Zurbaran', 'Sainte Casilda', *E*), the Crucifixion itself ('La Comédie de la Mort', III; 'Magdalena', *CM*) are neutralised emotionally by being interpreted in terms of decorative motifs. One recalls Baudelaire's eulogy of Gautier: 'Heureux homme! . . . il n'a aimé que le Beau . . . et quand un objet grotesque ou hideux s'est offert à ses yeux, il a su encore en extraire une mystérieuse et symbolique beauté!' (*BOC* 724). Religion itself offers irresistible aesthetic potential: Gautier values its colour, its art, its décor. His sacred characters display the same coquettishness and stylishness of pose as the poet relished in the heroines of Botticelli, Correggio and Parmigianino. Gautier's Virgins are indistinguishable from his Venuses; his Magdalena, set in a welter of *précieux* imagery, is seductive ('Magdalena', *CM*).[16]

The abuse of the decorative is indicative of Gautier's overwhelming desire—anticipating the Decadents—to see life itself as an aesthetic process. Experience is channelled into either actual or potential canvases or reduced to picturesque vignettes, reality is treated graphically or scenographically, and even when not consciously seeking the characteristic *transposition d'art*, his perception is organised into spatial relationships with flat, two-dimensional forms. The travel works frequently assimilate natural scenery to a stage backcloth, for with nature a jewel-case to be plundered by the artist-connoisseur the entire universe can easily become a theatre:

Par suite de ma concentration dans mon *ego*, cette idée m'est venue, maintes fois, que . . . le ciel, les astres, la terre, les maisons, les forêts, n'étaient que des décorations, des coulisses barbouillées à la brosse, que le mystérieux machiniste disposait autour de moi pour m'empêcher de voir les murs poudreux et pleins de toiles d'araignées de ce théâtre qu'on appelle le monde . . . ('Préface', *Les Jeunes-France*).

Nature must vie with man's decorative genius (flowers are particularly privileged) if it is not to be dismissed contemptuously as tawdry and inferior.[17]

Gautier's scenic imagery tends to crystallise around certain geometrical, linear motifs, of which the commonest are the angular (serrated skylines spiked with towers and angled roofs) and the sinuous which itself, identified with the caprice already defined, epitomises man's innate spirituality contemptuous of materiality. Like the flame, Gautier's arabesques, deriving from the *figura serpentinata* of Renaissance mannerism, defy matter and rise upwards to eternity.[18]

Architecture, as the one art by which man has most conspicuously left a permanent stamp on his environment, enjoys a privileged place in Gautier's affections, and the sheer incidence of architectural imagery is outstanding in his work. Once again, however, it is the peripheral decoration which fascinates him, and carving, mouldings, pattern and statuary are lovingly highlighted. The austerity of a church 'sans archanges sculptés, sans nervures ni frises' ('L'Horloge', *E*), is forbidding, while the gloomy Escorial is relieved from grotesqueness only by the capricious swallows nesting in its cornices ('L'Escurial', *E*; cf. 'Ce que disent les Hirondelles', *EC*).

Neglecting in practice, therefore, the classical virtues he favoured in theory, Gautier's visual imagination constantly escapes towards the floridness and the whimsicality of the rococo. Typified by Watteau's *fêtes galantes*, Marivaux's mannered graces and the fairy-like décor of Venice, 'ce joyeux dix-huitième siècle' ('Jean et Jeannette') is Gautier's spiritual home because of its sublimation of the decorative arts. His poetry, as well as his short stories, abounds in rococo motifs: mythological fancies, mirrors, textured costume, boudoir accessories, flora, shells, pastels, porcelain, trinkets, chinoiseries.

This type of visual *préciosité* receives perfect illustration in the frequency of images drawn from the ballet. Poetry and dance were sister arts for Gautier: both defy matter and are non-utilitarian, both are concerted artifice, supremely decorative, demanding 'un rythme oculaire'. Not only does his poetry depict many dancing figures (tritons and sea-nymphs, Hugo's Esmeralda and odalisques, classical Graces, Venus poised on the waves, Holbein's *danse macabre*, sabbaths and bacchanalia, Spanish cachuchas and seguidillas, Giselle in person . . .) but nature herself dances: poplars sway, dragonflies waltz, fountains arch, streams loop, seagulls pirouette, bats circle, smoke spirals. Often Gautier's heroines, all arabesques and poses with their dainty feet, swan's neck and 'taille cambrée' merge with ballerinas in their ultimate revelation of elusive grace.

Gautier's aesthetic of charm places a premium on delicacy, and one characteristic result is to make him a gifted miniaturist. Fearful of the amorphous totality of life, the poet takes refuge in contemplation of the diminutive, not only because daintiness has a curious intrinsic fascination and because the minute is easily confused with the refined but because detail reveals unforeseen uniqueness in the apparently familiar. The technique reflects Gautier's analytical mind, persuades him that art involves probing beneath grosser reality to discover elusive truths and enables him to view reality dispassionately, dissociated from any criteria other than formal.

His specialised use of light and colour stems from a similar search for the rare and refined. Gautier is an exceptionally luminous poet, a sun-worshipper with an instinctive dread of obscurity, for whom *grisâtre* was a term of abuse. A devotee of Hugo's *Les Orientales*, he over-indulges in spectacular effects of luminosity, either clear-cut black and white contrasts, chiaroscuro or—most typical of all—imagery of sparkle and glitter which studs his verse: dew, stars, moist eyes, sparkling snow, twinkling jewels, the shimmer of costume. Prismatic effects from the interplay of light and water are common in liquid imagery, while crystalline forms are another beautiful variant. Finally, for the poet who proclaimed 'la lumière est la forme du Verbe',[19] the novel *Spirite* demonstrates strikingly that for Gautier luminosity is not gratuitous prettiness but a metaphysical symbol.

Gautier's chromatic scale is equally idiosyncratic. Starting with an orgy of colour in reaction against neo-classic pallor he increasingly refines colour to its purest intensity, as in the sumptuous, heraldic tones of 'La Tulipe' (*DP*), or transmutes it into a quintessential whiteness of non-matter, symbolising an inaccessible perfection ('Symphonie en Blanc majeur', *EC*). Equally characteristic however is the symbolic use of muted tones, to suggest refinement, delicacy, intimacy, desire (rococo pinks) or the semi-mystical ideal of purity (azure).

Gautier's perception, though acute, is, in view of these conscious aberrations from objectivity, not that of a 'realist'. Far from photocopying reality, the poet's overwhelming decorative urge constantly reformulates it by the various processes we have enumerated—selection, fragmentation, miniaturism, stylisation—to create the heightened and enhanced reality we have termed the scenographic, offering him thereby a refuge from the insipidity of life.[20]

Absorbed in stylistic problems to an unusual degree Gautier attaches overriding importance to the poet's use of language, both in the narrow sense (choice and deployment of vocabulary, problems of rhyme) and the wider sense (conceits, metaphorism, general modes of expression). Contemptuous of what he regarded as the impoverished classical vocabulary, totally inadequate for modern artistic needs,[21] choice of vocabulary is determined for him by the criteria of intrinsic beauty and strangeness stressed in his eulogies of Banville and Baudelaire (see above, pp. 27-8). From such a philosophy of style results the frequently flamboyant nature of Gautier's poetic language. Technical vocabulary, proper nouns and foreign terms with their unique sonorities, picturesque archaisms, colloquialisms, word-play, oxymoron and ingenious rhymes all abound.

Much of the foregoing implies a somewhat cerebral, mechanical art of sophistry and ratiocination, illustrated by the adoption of a frequently argumentative, pseudo-dialectical manner:

> Mon cœur, ne battez plus, puisque vous êtes mort;
> ('Ténèbres', *CM*)

> Et qui, sachant l'effet dont la cause est suivie,
> Mélangent au présent l'avenir déjà vieux;
> ('L'Impassible', *DP*)

> Spectre dont le cadavre est vivant; ombre morte
> Que le passé ravit au présent qu'il emporte;
> Reflet dont le corps s'est enfui.
> ('Pensée de Minuit', *CM*)

Dependent on the same spirit of equivocation and whimsical speculation are innumerable *précieux* conceits around which entire poems may be constructed: 'Le Sonnet' (*DP*), 'Le Spectre de la Rose' (*CM*), 'A une Robe rose' (*EC*), 'La Mélodie et l'Accompagnement' (*DP*). Ingenious analogies revive the staple seventeenth century device of redefinition: a watch-spring is a 'papillon d'acier', while the butterfly in its turn is 'un page galant' or a 'blanche étincelle'. Eyelashes are seagulls poised for flight, snowy mountains are magistrates in ermine pondering a case, and the ordinary becomes fraught with magic:

> La lumière brisant dans chacun de mes cils,
> Palissade opposée à ses rayons subtils,
> Les sept couleurs du prisme . . .
>
> ('Far Niente', *P*)

Much of this type of imagery is traditional to *précieux* gallantry, like the many amorous conceits relating to prisons, tombs, eyes, tears, birds and fire.

Two wider modes of expression which go beyond the purely linguistic are antithesis, heightening and polarising experience, and hyperbole, which may be either a purely verbal, mechanical remnant from the poet's early 'paroxyste' phase,[22] or the more significant conceptual form of superlativism which seeks reassurance of perfection in a mediocre world. Gautier makes a cult of what has been termed 'edenism'[23]: everything tends to the archetypal in an idealised universe where things may yet happen for the first time, where 'la première des roses . . . Rit au premier beau jour' ('Tristesse', *CM*), and where heroines recall the *belle matineuse* of tradition (cf. 'Maria', *P*).

Such visual and verbal mannerisms are seen at their most characteristic when compressed into the rigid, tight-knit structures of the sonnet and the octosyllabic quatrain. The latter is a strongly restrictive form: the determinant of structure is so strong that there will be a tendency for octosyllabic verse to become a particular kind of verse in tone and ethos—the kind associated with the 'petits genres'—the fugitive and the delicately inconsequential, madrigals, romances. Gautier himself certainly associates it explicitly with 'de petits sujets' (cf. *HR* 322). With little *enjambement* possible if complete formlessness is to be avoided, each end-stopped line becomes a virtual entity. Clearly such a structure is peculiarly congenial to Gautier's poetic character: its overall rigidity demands compression, it highlights individual components like the isolated word, image or rhyme, tends to imprison rather than release the imagination which turns inwards in eddies of juxtaposed images, a process favoured by the crisscross rhyme. Adopted increasingly after *España*, the octosyllabic quatrain offers the poet a self-imposed formal refuge from facility and emotionalism; it is 'un défi au sentimentalisme'.[24]

Gautier's essentially eclectic art is a complex one which no single formula will adequately define. But it is arguable that, following Sainte-Beuve's remark about Gautier's unique 'manière' and in view of Gautier's defence of *marivaudage*,[25]—itself 'une nouvelle préciosité'[26]—what constitutes the single most recurrent constant in his poetry is the *précieux* spirit. It is not only that Gautier's poetics recall the Pléiade doctrine in major respects, that he admired Ronsard particularly (using 'ronsardiser' as synonymous with 'précieux'[27]), that he frequently plundered these poets for epigraphs,[28] that he pastiches *précieux* style in poetry and prose,[29] or that he regards the Renaissance madrigal as a personal ideal:

> Si comme Pétrarque et le vieux Ronsard,
> Viole d'amour ou lyre païenne,
> De fins concettis à l'italienne,
> Je savais orner un sonnet plein d'art;
> ('Modes et Chiffons', *DP*)

Gautier's whole concept of poetry establishes him firmly in the *précieux* tradition recurrent throughout French literature,[30] inspiring in him many entirely *précieux* compositions in each successive *recueil*.[31]

Admittedly the 'Parnassian' Gautier is able at times to achieve the harmony and serenity which he recurrently saw as one artistic ideal, magnificently expressed in the superb sonnet 'L'Impassible' (*DP*). More often, however, this statuesque Gautier is submerged by more restless, capricious forces resulting in the luxuriant ornamentation, the display of fanciful patterns, the whimsical speculation and the unashamed pursuit of the charming which we have noted constantly in both poetry and prose, and which are epitomised by his concept of the 'caprice'. Indulgence towards caprice, Gautier believes (cf. *Les Grotesques*, 1), is the peculiar virtue of 'secondary' artists, less constrained than their great contemporaries. Such a 'grotesque' spirit, he notes approvingly, is still alive in authors such as Baudelaire or Banville, or in a contemporary artist like Froment Meurice:

Il a su varier à l'infini ces créations fantasques du monde de l'ornement où la femme jaillit du calice de la fleur, où la chimère se termine en feuillage, où la salamandre se tord dans un feu de rubis, où le lézard fuit sous des herbes d'émeraude, où l'arabesque embrouille à plaisir ses entrelacs et ses complications . . . (*HR* 242).

The 'arabesque', associated with sinuous gothic decoration (cf. 'Portail', *CM*), is, however, equally applicable to a type of poetry or prose dependent on extravagant conceits:

. . . en dehors des compositions que l'on peut appeler classiques . . . il existe un genre auquel conviendrait assez le nom d'arabesque, où, sans grand souci de la pureté des lignes, le crayon s'égaye en mille fantaisies baroques . . . les plus gens de goût ont besoin quelquefois, pour se remettre en appétit, du piment de concetti et des gongorismes.

('Préface', *Les Grotesques*)

Such whimsical sinuosity is then further related to literary *préciosité*:

. . . la préciosité la plus exquise pousse à droite et à gauche ses vrilles capricieuses et ses fleurs bizarres aux parfums enivrants—la préciosité, cette belle fleur française . . .

(Ibid., ix)

Gautier is thus ultimately less 'classical' or Parnassian in spirit than baroque or rococo, and it is here that the properly *précieux* spirit with its interplay of frivolity and reason, its unresolved tensions between two irreconcilable yet fundamental artistic needs—necessity of order and free play of fancy—its apparent gratuitousness, are most evident.

'*Apparent* gratuitousness': for if it is accepted that play in children and animals is purposeful, the same principle must apply to the peculiar brand of frivolity presented by much of Gautier's work. When Shakespeare's King Richard chides the dying Gaunt for inappropriate levity the old man retorts: 'Misery makes sport to mock itself' (*Richard II*, ii, i); and Gautier's remark 'Nous rions, —parce que nous ne pouvons pleurer' (*MM* 117) invites us to view his work as a kind of desperate therapy. Indeed, it is possible to go further. One modern critic, for example, has argued that *préciosité*, far from being frivolous, is an essentially 'heroic' posture vis-à-vis the mediocrity inherent in the human condition,[32] while another agrees that 'la préciosité proteste contre l'impureté de l'existence', is an act of defiance constituting 'une exigence métaphysique'.[33] Such arguments are all the more suggestive in view of Gautier's fervent idealism and his stress on art as 'une création dans une création', superior to the 'real' world, in which each fragmented, minute particle is potentially significant.

Ultimately however, the artist is none the less deeply aware, as we have noted, of his impotence, recognising the impossibility of attaining 'truth', and the result in Gautier's case is not only the recurrent irony, paradoxes and tensions but a pervading sense o mystery emanating from the objects of the external world. Gautier is deeply conscious of the 'otherness' of things and of the impenetrability of time and space relationships, which are constantly blurred. Rimbaud acknowledged, in the celebrated letter to Demeny of 15 May 1871, Gautier's talent for resurrecting the inanimate ('reprendre l'esprit des choses mortes'), while Gautier himself, in a striking formula, proclaims: 'le poète a, comme la pythonesse d'Endor, la puissance de faire apparaître et parler les ombres'.[34] Gautier's Hoffmannesque stories richly illustrate this tendency, as we have already seen.

Baudelaire went a stage further, however, when he analysed Gautier's supernaturalism, observing perceptively that Gautier defines 'l'attitude mystérieuse que les objets de la création tiennent devant le regard de l'homme' (*BOC* 690), and this mystery is translated by the frequent images of mutation which, assuming often a peculiar resonance, remind us of the fundamental ambiguities of the universe of 'contours équivoques' (*A*, xi) which surround us. The metamorphosis—itself one of *préciosité*'s staple genres (cf. Voiture's celebrated 'Métamorphose de Julie en diamant')—is a two-way process with many variations. On the one hand, petrification, crystallisation, suspended animation, reduction of the living to plastic, stylised postures abound; on the other hand, dissolution, humanisation of the inanimate, reanimation of the inert, the dead, the past into the fluidity of life, are all equally common. Particularly characteristic of Gautier are images of arrested movement, evoking life mysteriously poised between the two states:

> Les blanches dentelles des vasques,
> Pleurs de l'ondine en l'air figés;
> ('Symphonie en blanc majeur', *EC*),

Impéria's hand, 'sous le baiser neigeux saisie' ('Etude de Mains', *EC*), flowers transformed into 'des papillons peureux suspendus dans leur vol' ('Le Triomphe de Pétrarque', *CM*); winter which,

> Dans ses rêts froids et tenaces
>   . . .
> Et se durcissant en glaces,
> Fige le poisson dans l'eau.
>   ('La Neige', *DP*)

Such processes suggest, half-flippantly, half-seriously, the infinite interchangeability of things, and this parallelism is a kind of poetic double-talk deriving basically from the Renaissance doctrine of occult correspondences, a secret intuition of which, explains Gautier in his 1868 essay on *Les Fleurs du Mal*, is the prerogative of the true poet. Nature, 'ce grand livre où la plume divine/Ecrit le grand secret que nul œil ne devine' ('Départ', *E*), performs a constant 'acte de mystère' ('Tombée du Jour', *CM*). The universe is a cypher, its intractability recalled by numerous sphinxes. For the deeply superstitious devotee of Hoffmann nothing is permanently static or inert: 'l'air frémit, l'eau soupire et semble avoir une âme' ('L'Ondine et le Pêcheur', *PN*), 'le marbre ému sent sa fraîcheur' ('Affinités Secrètes', *EC*), 'l'albâtre s'attendrit et fond en blanches larmes' ('Portail', *CM*). Hence the peculiar resonance of Gautier's liquid imagery: rivulets, rainbows, water-drops, tears, fountains—all favourites with the early mannerists. It is an analogical universe in which potentially everything has occult relation with everything else, and in which mutability is a cosmic law:

> Marbre, perle, rose, colombe,
> Tout se dissout, tout se détruit;
> La perle fond, le marbre tombe,
> La fleur se fane et l'oiseau fuit.
>   ('Affinités Secrètes', *EC*'

Again,

> Arbre ou tombeau, colombe ou rose,
>   Onde ou rocher,
> Tout, ici-bas, a quelque chose
>   Pour s'épancher . . .
>   ('Dans un baiser, l'onde . . .', *PN*)

Such processes, so constant as to inspire an endless stream of beautiful and suggestive images, are clearly more than a poetic trick. They are evidence that, however obscurely, Gautier is attempting to express his perception of spiritual resonances in nature. Attuned to the mysterious inner life of the universe, impressed by the revelation of the second *Faust*,[35] the poet attempts to pierce the opacity of things (one recalls Mallarmé's phrase in his eulogy of Gautier, 'Toast Funèbre', about the poet's 'regard diaphane'), becoming an 'œil qui sait voir les larmes des choses' ('A Ernest Hébert', *DP*), deciphering 'quel sens ont les soupirs qui dans les bois s'élèvent' ('Perplexité', *DP*).

The truth is that, marvelling at Hugo's capacity to record 'le chuchotement mystérieux de l'infini' (*HR* 396) and acknowledged as a *voyant* by fellow poets (cf. pp. 94–5), Gautier anticipates to a considerable extent the most characteristic features of symbolism through his insistence that art must go beyond the surface, 'chercher quelque chose au-delà de ce qui est'.[36]

The 'symbolist' Gautier is seen, not of course in the somewhat laboured romantic symbols of the early allegories of *La Comédie de la Mort* (cf. 'Le Pot de Fleurs', 'Choc de Cavaliers', 'Le Sphinx'), whose explicitness and coherence exclude true poetic suggestion, but in the wayward, musical element of the same volume's romances (see above, pp. 53–4), the elusiveness of compositions like 'Le Spectre de la Rose', 'Les Colombes', 'Rocaille', 'Watteau', 'Tombée du Jour', and, above all, in the fundamentally mystical concept of his art. Already, the hero of *Mademoiselle de Maupin* was unable to live in the same dimension as others—anticipating Malivert's dilemma in *Spirite*—and it is in the poetic act of transposing his being outside the dimensions of space and time that Gautier's true affinities with the symbolists are apparent. This transmigration, already the subject of much of his fiction, is achieved for Gautier through the medium of his senses which recapture the rapturous feeling of the infinite, drawing man away from material reality. Form itself is neither concrete nor explicit, but elusive, hauntingly reminiscent of a glimpsed eternity:

Sous la forme *exprimée* on sent une pensée vague, infinie, *inexprimable*, comme une idée musicale; on est ému, troublé; des images *déjà vues* vous passent devant les yeux, des voix dont on croit reconnaître le timbre vous chuchotent à l'oreille de langoureuses confidences; les désirs réprimés, les espérances qui désespéraient s'agitent douloureusement dans une ombre mêlée de rayons . . .[37]

Gautier 'éprouve un obscur pressentiment des réalités invisibles', writes Castex in his study of the *Contes fantastiques*, and any medium—love, religious ecstasy, art, drugs (which in 1843 had given him his first vivid experience of synaesthesia)[38]—is valid which enables man to penetrate momentarily this extraterrestrial dimension. Gautier wrote:

La croyance aux apparitions n'est donc qu'un corollaire de l'immortalité de l'âme et une vague aperception du monde aromal qui nous entoure, et que nous ne pouvons découvrir sans être dans des conditions de vision particulière.[39]

Constantly aspiring to that mysterious spiritual essence of the universe which alone sustains it and releases the artist from exile in the material world, the poetic vision acquires a prophetic quality:

> C'est à cette heure-là que les divins poètes
> Sentent grandir leur front et deviennent prophètes.
> ('Magdalena', *CM*)

Art thereby becomes an almost magic conquest and, in Mallarmé's celebrated definition, 'doue ainsi d'authenticité notre séjour . . . seule tâche spirituelle'.[40] Scoffing at Gautier's 'cécité pour tout ce qui n'est pas le monde extérieur',[41] Gide's judgement is quite obtuse. Paradoxically, the 'surface' Gautier yields constantly to the transcendentalism of Spirite who,

. . . avec une intuition merveilleuse, rendait l'au-delà des mots, le non-sorti du verbe humain, ce qui reste inédit dans la phrase la mieux faite, le mystérieux, l'intime, et le profond des choses.[42]

Gautier himself admitted, in a characteristic paradox, that 'je n'ai pas le degré de stupidité nécessaire pour devenir ce que l'on appelle absolument un *génie*' (*MM* 260). Nevertheless, his concern to avoid the bogus element in romanticism, his obligation to be true to his own vision and sensibility, ought to command respect in the modern age, with its impatience with what Gautier termed *cant.* The poet must be judged by the ways in which he handles his own conception of art, by the honesty which led him to act upon the realisation of his peculiar talent, and by the courage with which he so effectively challenged previous artistic suppositions. For Gautier, unlike the romantics, the poem is a caprice, a kind of ingenious ceremony or *divertissement*, apposite and decorative rather than cathartic. He never intended his art to be true in the sense of being recognisably like 'life' or wished it to relate directly to the human predicament. Art was rather the exploration of a self-contained world emancipated from actuality and contingency. Naïve as a child's, his imagination was also as intense, but it does not therefore follow that this intensity should pass into his work. For he strove constantly in his maturity to conceal the pain which the bleakness and mediocrity of life caused him, choosing rather to express with deceptive simplicity something of the magic and also the mystery of the world about and within us.

VII

SOME VIEWS ON GAUTIER

Poésies (1830, 1832)

C'est l'animation, c'est le souffle qui manquent surtout aux compositions de M. Gautier. La faute en est peut-être à sa trop grande préoccupation de la forme et de la rime . . . Le savoir-faire et le talent sont incontestables dans ce livre, mais, disons-le, l'originalité n'est pas là.

> *Les Débats*, 1 November 1830. (The first known review of Gautier's work.)

M. Gautier se recommande surtout par ce que j'appellerai le matériel de la poésie: il hasarde souvent des mots, des phrases, des coupes d'une rare et merveilleuse originalité. Mais son expression bizarre manque de force et de vie; ses tableaux colorés avec tant de soin n'ont pas assez d'âme et de chaleur; l'esprit se fatigue à travers les détails dont il abonde, et cherche en vain une pensée unique . . .

> *L'Artiste*, 1832.

Les Jeunes-France (1833)

L'auteur jetait le sarcasme sur toute chose avec profusion: son allure dégagée et impertinente, ses idées paradoxales, sa manière d'écrire, si originale et si amusante, lui valurent l'amitié d'une foule de jeunes gens . . .

> *La France littéraire*, 1836.

'Villon', *Les Grotesques* (1834)

A quel degré de dépravation le goût et la morale sont-ils arrivés pour qu'on ose signer un pareil article et pour qu'une feuille périodique ose le publier?

> *Le Constitutionnel*, 31 May 1834.

Mademoiselle de Maupin (1835–6)

L'esprit de M. Gautier est doué d'une originalité vraie et qui le met à part; en toute chose il a horreur du commun, du banal, du convenu. En toute chose il cherche le côté choisi, élégant, spirituel, paradoxal, singulier, quelquefois étrange, la face aperçue de peu de regards. Il incline au fantastique, mais au fantastique lumineux ... au fantastique rabelaisien, au fantastique de l'ancienne comédie italienne ...

> Victor Hugo, *Le Vert-Vert*, 15 December 1835.

Adorateur de la forme et de la beauté plastique, [Gautier] redemande aux Grecs et aux Romains cette fierté de pinceau, cette transparence de chair, cette correction et cette hardiesse de lignes, cet amour des détails, cette richesse du style dont les modernes semblent avoir perdu le secret ... L'auteur parle cette belle langue de Louis XIII, si fière, si empanachée, si grande dame ... Le style, quoique ordinairement ferme et robuste, se prend çà et là aux préciosités et aux mignardises de Watteau avec un art et un bonheur inouïs ...

> A. Esquiros, *La Presse*, 14 October 1836.

... un livre magnifique, *Mademoiselle de Maupin*, où M. Gautier est entré, fouet en main, éperonné, botté comme Louis XIV à son fameux lit de justice, au plein cœur du journalisme. Cette œuvre de verve comique, disons mieux, cet acte de courage a prouvé le danger de l'entreprise. Le livre, une des plus artistes, des plus verdoyantes, des plus pimpantes, des plus vigoureuses compositions de notre époque, d'une allure si vive, d'une tournure si contraire au commun de nos livres, a-t-il eu tout son succès? en a-t-on suffisamment parlé?

> Balzac, 'Préface', *Un Grand Homme de Province à Paris*, 1839.

L'auteur y donne à boire le poison dans une coupe de diamant ... Il déploie l'étendard de la débauche la plus ignoble de toutes, celle qui n'a même pas d'excuse dans la nature ... M. Gautier a fait plus qu'un mauvais livre, il a commis une mauvaise action ... Qu'un jeune homme au sortir du collège, qu'une fille de quinze ans viennent à feuilleter une de ces pages, ils seront démoralisés jusqu'à la moelle des os.

E. de Mirecourt, *Théophile Gautier*, Roret, 1856.

Par son style prodigieux, par sa beauté correcte et recherché, pure et fleurie, ce livre était un véritable événement . . . Avec *Mademoiselle de Maupin* apparaissait dans la littérature le Dilettantisme qui, par son caractère exquis et superlatif, est toujours la meilleure preuve des facultés indispensables en art. Ce roman, ce conte, ce tableau, cette rêverie continuée avec l'obstination d'un peintre, cette espèce d'hymne à la Beauté, avait ce grand résultat d'établir définitivement la condition génératrice des œuvres d'art, c'est-à-dire l'amour exclusif du Beau, l'*Idée fixe*.

Baudelaire, *L'Artiste*, 13 March 1859.

Emaux et Camées (1852)

Emaux et Camées, quel titre fin, curieux, agaçant pour l'œil des poètes et des artistes . . . Th. Gautier a une prédilection pour le vers de huit pieds; c'est le mètre par excellence des joailleries du style; il découpe l'image, il multiplie les tailles, il a le son net, fréquent et clair du marteau du ciseleur repoussant une figure ou raffinant un relief.

Paul de Saint-Victor, *Le Pays*, 26 July 1852.

Il y a enfin une âme ici, une âme ingénue et émue dans cet homme voué, disait-il, au procédé! . . . Son titre est vaincu par son livre! Ce titre ne dit pas la moitié du livre qu'il nomme. Il en dit le côté étincelant et sec. Il n'en dit pas le côté noyé, voilé et tendre.

Barbey d'Aurevilly, *Les Œuvres et les Hommes*, Amyot, 1862.

Désormais rien ni pour le cœur ni pour la pensée. Des formes bien vues et bien dessinées . . . voilà le dernier terme où devait atteindre . . . cet art prodigieusement artificiel . . .

E. Faguet, *Dix-Neuvième Siècle, Etudes littéraires*, Boivin, 1887.

Ce petit recueil de vers est un joyau de la langue française . . . L'artiste s'y est mis tout entier, avec son culte de la beauté plastique, traduite par le marbre ou la chair, ses extases devant les souples contours et les attitudes harmonieuses, . . . enfin son dilettantisme et sa virtuosité.

H. Potez, *Théophile Gautier*, Armand Colin, 1903.

GENERAL JUDGEMENTS

On ne tarde pas à s'apercevoir que le procédé de l'auteur ne se conforme pas toujours au sujet, n'est pas . . . proportionné à l'idée ou au sentiment, qu'il y a parti pris dans le mode d'expression exclusivement tourné à la couleur et à l'image . . . Est-ce l'image qui fait loi? . . . Ici, chez M. Gautier, l'eau ne court que sous une surface glacée et miroitante au soleil . . . entre vous et le sentiment, au lieu du libre cours s'interpose cette glace d'images ininterrompue et peinte en mille tons . . . à la longue, cela fait trop l'effet d'une verroterie.

Sainte-Beuve, *Revue des Deux Mondes*, 15 September 1838.

Si l'on réfléchit qu'à cette merveilleuse faculté Gautier unit une immense intelligence innée de la *correspondance* et du symbolisme universels, ce répertoire de toute métaphore, on comprendra qu'il puisse sans cesse . . . définir l'attitude mystérieuse que les objets de la création tiennent devant le regard de l'homme. Il y a dans le mot, dans le *verbe*, quelque chose de *sacré* qui nous défend d'en faire un jeu de hasard. Manier savamment une langue, c'est pratiquer une espèce de sorcellerie évocatoire.

Baudelaire, *L'Artiste*, 13 March 1859.

Il y a donc deux existences dans son existence, deux œuvres dans son œuvre: l'un subtil, perspicace, modéré . . . l'autre excessif, énorme, sans frein par le côté création, touffu, plein d'ardeurs, de rêveries, de spontanéité, prodigieux par la variété, durable par la diversité et la précision des connaissances, qui s'y cachent sous la grâce et la perfection du style comme sous des fleurs.

C. Yriarte, *Les Portraits Cosmopolites*, Lachaud, 1870.

Gautier fut très peu romantique, très peu féru du moyen âge, car il y eut toujours en lui l'amour de la vie, de la beauté pure et sereine, des lignes idéales, comme l'entendait l'antiquité hellénique, l'adoration des golfes d'azur et des lauriers-roses, et en même temps la gaieté, la saine ironie, le clair et net esprit français des vieux conteurs et de Voltaire.

Théodore de Banville, Speech at Inauguration of monument to Gautier, 25 June 1875.

The beauty and variety of our present earth and the insatiability of our earthly temperament were his theme, and . . . he brought to his task a sort of pagan *bonhomie* . . . he was a sort of immeasurably lighter-handed Rabelais.

Henry James, *French Poets and Novelists*, Macmillan, 1878.

Aucune idée nouvelle apportée, aucune vérité humaine de quelque profondeur, aucune prescience de l'évolution des siècles; rien que des symphonies exécutées sur les lieux communs qui courent nos ateliers et nos cabinets d'artistes depuis 1830. Toute l'œuvre écrite ou parlée de ce poète a été une gymnastique étourdissante sur le terrain du paradoxe . . . On a été charmé peut-être, mais on n'a pas été instruit. De là, le vide absolu de son œuvre.

Zola, *Le Messager de l'Europe*, July 1879.

Celui-ci est un génie étroit, absolument original et de premier ordre dans les limites de sa puissance . . . Il était venu à la poésie par un atelier de peintre: et il ne fut jamais qu'un peintre fourvoyé dans la littérature . . . sans idées ni émotions, il a rendu les fragments du monde extérieur qui tombaient sous son expérience . . . Son exactitude de peintre ou de graveur l'a fait sortir du romantisme: il a renoncé au lyrisme subjectif pour s'asservir à l'objet.

G. Lanson, *Histoire de la littérature française*, Hachette, 1894.

. . . Gautier occupe une place considérable; c'est seulement fâcheux qu'il la remplisse si mal.

André Gide, Lecture, 1914, reprinted in *Incidences*, Gallimard, 1924.

La poésie de Gautier est . . . *une poésie d'oubli dans le charme de l'apparence.*

> G. Brunet, 'Théophile Gautier poète', *Mercure de France,* 15 October 1922.

Il resta toute sa vie un romantique de l'école des Tristan l'Hermite, des Saint-Amant, des Théophile de Viau, des Corneille, des Scudéry et des Scarron, c'est-à-dire de la France héroïque, burlesque et précieuse du XVIIe siècle . . . Il a comme les grotesques . . . cette imagination particulière, d'essence plastique, ce goût, à la fois réaliste et chimérique, qui les incite à *artialiser la nature* plutôt qu'à *naturaliser l'art,* selon le mot de Montaigne.

> J. Charpentier, 'La réaction parnassienne', *Mercure de France,* 15 March 1925.

Gautier trouve donc une exaltation lyrique à s'éblouir de vie, à s'enivrer d'émotions rapides, de certitude plastique, de sensualité et de rythme païen.

> Antoine-Orliac, 'Essai sur le pessimisme chez les Parnassiens', *Mercure de France,* 15 August 1928.

Ce qui domine chez Gautier, c'est la hantise de la mort . . . Rien ne devait paraître plus intolérable à Gautier que cette aperception simultanée de l'"éternelle beauté' et de l'éternel travail de dissolution qui en accompagne la présence. L'objet sensible se découvrait à la fois, en même temps, comme éternel et transitoire, comme inaltérable et s'altérant.

> G. Poulet, *Etudes sur le temps humain,* Plon, 1949.

Son univers est celui de ces précieux, excentriques ou burlesques, qu'il appelait naguère les *Grotesques* du XVIIe siècle . . . Mais voici que cette ingéniosité de précieux l'entraîne au-delà de son art plastique, charge d'intentions et de pensée cette peinture . . . De là, un prolongement subtil et indéfini de la vision; le tableau plastique et net s'achève en musique, en rêve; des correspondances mystérieuses relient les couleurs, les sensations, les désirs, les regrets . . . Gautier qui . . . est le maître du Parnasse, mène aussi, par une voie détournée, au symbolisme.

P. Moreau, *Le Romantisme*, Del Duca, 1957.

Gautier 'maître et ombre' est un écrivain d'avenir, non pas tant parce qu'il fut un poète impeccable, que parce que son angoisse sut se masquer sous les dehors de l'humour et du fantastique.

L. Cellier, *Nouvelles Littéraires*, November 1972.

NOTES

PREFACE

1. 'Théophile Gautier', *Revue fantaisiste*, 15 July 1861, reprinted in *L'Art romantique* in 1869. Cf. *BOC* 722.
2. Cf. respectively, the contributions of Dierx and Aubanel to *Le Tombeau de Théophile Gautier*, Lemerre, 1873.
3. Cf. *EB* 57, 63, 72, 207; and see below, p. 129, n. 96.
4. *Axel's Castle*, Fontana Library, Collins, 1961, p. 13.
5. Victor Hugo, 'A Théophile Gautier' (*Toute la Lyre*).

LIFE

1. The unique source for Gautier's early life is R. Jasinski, *Les Années Romantiques de Th. Gautier*, Vuibert, 1929. For a complete biography, see J. Richardson, *Théophile Gautier, His Life and Times*, Reinhardt, 1958.
2. Cf. Maxime du Camp, *Théophile Gautier*, Hachette, 1919, p. 184.
3. To Nerval Gautier owed his first poetic attempts, his initiation into German thought and literature (especially through Nerval's translations of *Faust*), an interest in the occult, a taste for eighteenth-century art, and the crucial introduction to Victor Hugo.
4. Gautier's autobiographical sketch first appeared in *L'Illustration*, 9 March 1867, then in *Portraits Contemporains* (1874), before being reprinted as 'Gautier par lui-même' in A. Boschot's *Théophile Gautier: Souvenirs Romantiques*, Garnier, 1929.
5. Cf. the valuable chapter 'Théophile Gautier peintre', in *EB*, followed by a catalogue of Gautier's drawings and paintings. Some of these are reproduced in J. Tild, *Théophile Gautier et ses amis*, Albin Michel, 1951.
6. Cf. *HR* x–xii; also E. de Goncourt's 'Préface' in *EB* v–vi.
7. Cf. the famous 'Sonnet de l'Eléphant' ('Sonnet vii', *P*) and Jasinski's comments, *AR* 80–1; also 'Préface', *Les Jeunes-France*: 'Qu'est-ce qu'une révolution . . .?'
8. See the amusing accounts in *HR* ii, iii, etc.
9. Cf. Nerval's *Petits Châteaux de Bohème*, Champion, 1926; *AR* viii; J. Richardson, *The Bohemians*, Macmillan, 1969; S. O. Simches, *Le Romantisme et le Goût esthétique du XVIIIe siècle*, PUF, 1964; and *POC* 234 ff., 268, etc.

10. The artists included, notably, Chassériau and J.-B. Corot. Gautier himself contributed an 'imitation d'un Watteau ou d'un Lancret quelconque' (*POC* 237).

11. Cf. the moving letter to his sisters, 17 December 1858, reprinted in P. Descaves, *Les Plus Belles Lettres de Théophile Gautier*, Calmann-Lévy, 1962, pp. 76–9.

12. Cf. A. Boschot, *Théophile Gautier*, Desclée de Brouwer, 1933, p. 72.

13. *RDDM*, 1 April 1841.

14. *Le Moniteur Universel*, 29 September 1856, quoted in *JE* 65.

15. Private dedication to Nestor Roqueplan, the dandy of the Doyenné community. Cf. *HR* 174–8.

16. Published 16, 23 and 30 November 1863 in *Le Constitutionnel*, and reprinted in *Nouveaux Lundis*, Michel Lévy, 1875, VI. Sainte-Beuve had devoted two earlier articles to Gautier, in *RDDM*, 15 September 1838 and *RDP*, 31 October 1844.

17. Gautier's own term, according to E. de Goncourt, 'Préface', *EB* XVII.

18. Cf. J. Tild, op. cit., p. 203; J. Richardson, *Théophile Gautier*, op. cit., pp. 218–19 and *La Vie parisienne*, 1852–70, Hamilton, 1971, p. 61.

19. E. de Goncourt, 'Préface', *EB* XX–XXI.

20. Ibid., XIV–XV.

AESTHETIC DOCTRINE

1. G. Matoré, *La Préface de 'Mademoiselle de Maupin'*, Droz, 1946, p. xliv.

2. Article on R. Töpffer. 'Du Beau dans l'Art', *RDDM*, 1 July 1847 (hereafter referred to as 'Töpffer').

3. Ibid; and *L'Artiste*, 5 September 1858: 'espèce de *desideratum* de l'infini, de vague aspiration à l'idéal, de souvenir inconscient d'un état antérieur'.

4. Ibid: 'c'est presque une idée innée . . .'

5. Cf. *POC* 241–3.

6. For the microcosm concept, see Gautier's articles in *La Presse*, 4 April 1839; in *RDP*, April 1841; on Delacroix in *Le Moniteur Universel*, 19 July 1855 and 18 November 1864 (reprinted in *HR*); in *L'Artiste*, 18 January 1857; on Balzac in *L'Artiste*, 1858 (in *SR*); on G. Doré in *L'Artiste*, 20 December 1857; etc. For discussion, cf. A. Boschot's edition of *Emaux et Camées*, Garnier, 1954, pp. xxxvii–xli, and M. C. Spencer, *The Art Criticism of Théophile Gautier*, Droz, 1969, pp. 15–19, 98, 109–13, etc.

7. Conclusion of Töpffer article. The relationship between beauty and

truth was widely discussed in the eighteenth century (it forms, for example, the central theme of Schiller's *Die Künstler*, 1789). Gautier's important Töpffer article is much indebted to eighteenth-century German aesthetics. See below, p. 126, n. 40.

8. Article in *L'Artiste*, 13 March 1859, later incorporated into *L'Art romantique*. (*BOC* 680).

9. For Gautier's views on relative beauty, cf. his articles in *La Presse*, 21 April 1848, 7 August 1849 and 27 May 1852. Cf. M. C. Spencer's comments, op. cit., pp. 13–14, 41–2.

10. Töpffer.

11. *MM* 194.

12. *A*, LVIII; and 'Excellence de la Poésie', *Fusains et Eaux-Fortes*, Charpentier, 1880, p. 54.

13. *La Presse*, 29 November 1847.

14. Letter to Sainte-Beuve, 12 October 1857, quoted in Lovenjoul, op. cit., I, xix–xx.

15. 'Compensation', *CM*.

16. *RDDM*, 1 April 1841.

17. Cf. 'L'Hippogriffe, Sonnet 1' (*DP*), 'Les Souhaits' (*P*), etc. An old concept, common in the eighteenth century: cf. M. Gilman, *The Idea of Poetry in France*, Harvard, 1958, p. 23.

18. Letter to Sainte-Beuve, 12 October 1857, quoted in Lovenjoul, op. cit., I, xix–xx.

19. Cf. 'Ténèbres', 'Terza Rima', *CM*.

20. Töpffer.

21. *Fusains et Eaux-Fortes*, p. 48.

22. 'A Mme Marguerite Dardenne de la Grangerie' (Sonnet II), (*DP*).

23. 'Consolation' (*E*); cf. also 'Le Poète et la Foule', 'Perspective' (*E*), etc.

24. *POC* 201.

25. 'Consolation' (*E*). See Jasinski's comments, *PC* I, LXXVII.

26. Article on Berlioz's *Roméo et Juliette*, *La Presse*, 11 December 1839, quoted in *PC* I, LXXVII.

27. 'Chapelain', *Les Grotesques*, Desessart, 1844, II, p. 97.

28. *POC* 443.

29. *HR* 155.

30. 'A Jean Duseigneur', *DP*.

31. *HR* 156.

32. Töpffer.

33. Cf. *La Presse*, 20 March and 22 April 1848; *L'Artiste*, February 1858.

34. *L'Artiste*, February 1858.

35. *RDDM*, 1 April 1841.

36. *POC* 226.

37. *L'Artiste*, September 1858.

38. 'Notice' to *Les Fleurs du Mal*, Michel Lévy, 1868, reprinted in *SR* 300–1.

39. *Le Moniteur Universel*, 5 September 1860, and *Guide de l'Amateur au Musée du Louvre*, Charpentier, 1882, p. 177.

40. Kant's aesthetics had, via Hegel, Goethe, Schiller, etc., been proclaimed in France by Mme de Staël and Constant, the latter using the term 'l'art pour l'art' in connection with Kant as early as 1804 (*Journaux Intimes*). Further propagated by Cousin's Sorbonne lectures of 1818, these ideas became fashionable among the French romantics, themselves uneasy over political and social pressures. The precise extent of Gautier's knowledge of German aesthetics is debatable, but his frequent contact with Nerval and Heine, each extremely informed about German thought, must have been crucial. Cf. the article by J. Wilcox in *Journal of Aesthetics and Art Criticism*, XI, June 1953 for the general question; and, for specific channels, F. Baldensperger, *Goethe en France*, Hachette, 1904, E. Eggli, *Schiller et le Romantisme français*, 2 vols., Gamber, 1927, and F. Hirth, *Heinrich Heine und seine französischen Freunde*, Mainz, Florian Kupferberg Verlag, 1949.

41. Cf. G. V. Plekhanov, *Art and Social Life*, Lawrence and Wishart, 1953, pp. 174, 193, etc.; and A. Hauser, *Mannerism*, Routledge, 1965.

402. *POC* 289.

43. *L'Artiste*, 14 December 1856.

44. Töpffer. The poet is like the sun, shining indifferently on 'charogne' and 'rose'. Cf. Gautier's comments on Baudelaire's 'Le Soleil', (*SR* 300).

45. Töpffer. Cf. Gautier in *Le Figaro*, 11 November 1836.

46. Cf. 'Du Beau antique et du Beau moderne', *L'Evénement*, 8 August 1848, later reprinted as 'Plastique de la Civilisation' in *Souvenirs de Théâtre, d'Art et de Critique*, Charpentier, 1883.

47. Cf. Ibid; and J. Richardson, *Théophile Gautier*, pp. 130–3; M. C. Spencer, op. cit., pp. 25, 43, etc., and H. van der Tuin, *L'Evolution psychologique, esthétique et littéraire de Théophile Gautier*, Amsterdam, 1933, pp. 248 ff.

48. *L'Orient*, Charpentier, 1877, I, p. 352.

49. Gautier, as quoted by Houssaye in *Les Confessions, Souvenirs d'un demi-siècle*, 1830–80, Dentu, 1885–91, IV, p. 289. Cf. articles in *La Presse*, 20 March and 22 April 1848.

50. The value of the term 'artificial' has become inverted. Wholly complimentary in the sixteenth century, it was already pejorative by Gautier's time. Gautier, on the contrary, noted admiringly Baudelaire's

'sentiment de l'*artificiel*' (*SR* 309, 295–6), seeing this as a keynote of modern 'decadence'.

51. Oscar Wilde, 'The Decay of Lying', *Intentions*, Osgood, 1891, pp. 1–2. Cf. below, p. 139, n. 38.

52. *Salon de 1837*.

53. 'Pochades et Paradoxes', *Caprices et Zigzags*, Hachette, 1856, vii, p. 206.

54. 'Utilité de la Poésie', *Fusains et Eaux-Fortes*, p. 214.

55. Töpffer.

56. 'Statues de Michel-Ange', *Fusains et Eaux-Fortes*, p. 138.

57. *Le Moniteur Universel*, 5 September 1860; cf. also *Guide de l'Amateur au Musée du Louvre*, pp. 176–9.

58. *Le Moniteur Universel*, 5 September 1860; cf. also ibid., 1 April 1862. For Boucher and Fragonard, cf. *Guide de l'Amateur au Musée du Louvre*, pp. 180–4.

59. *L'Orient*, i, p. 352.

60. *POC* 341; the whole article is a defence of scenography. Cf. E. Souffrin, 'Banville et la Poétique du Décor', in *French Nineteenth Century Painting and Literature*, ed. U. Finke, Manchester University Press, 1972.

61. Cf. H. Patch, *The Dramatic Criticism of Théophile Gautier*, Bryn Mawr, 1922. His ideal theatre (cf. *MM* 241–8) will avoid reality, exploit the fanciful and create a world of poetic illusion by use of 'la féerie' (cf. *Journal Officiel*, 18 August 1869). The version of *As You Like It* in *MM* ch. xi is notable as the first major recognition in France given to Shakespeare's comedies. In a sense, Gautier's ideal theatre finds its truest expression in his ballets, veritable 'poèmes dansés' (*EB* 84). Cf. E. Binney, *Les Ballets de Théophile Gautier*, Nizet, 1965, and E. Souffrin, 'Théodore de Banville et le ballet romantique', *RSH* January–March 1963.

62. 'Utilité de la Poésie' and 'Statues de Michel-Ange', *Fusains et Eaux-Fortes*. Cf. 'La Toison d'Or' (in *Nouvelles*, Charpentier, 1889, p. 196: 'faire une création à part dans la créaton de Dieu').

63. Töpffer. Cf. *VE* 61 and *C* 326.

64. Cf. 'Celle-Ci et Celle-Là', in *Les Jeunes-France* (Charpentier, 1881, p. 305): 'la poésie, toute fille du ciel qu'elle est, n'est pas dédaigneuse des choses les plus humbles . . .'

65. *La Presse*, 17 March 1837 and RDP, April 1841.

66. 'Réflexions sur quelques-uns de mes contemporains' (*BOC* 724).

67. Cf. Gautier's analysis of the 'grotesque' principles in *Les Grotesques*, Desessart, 1844 (e.g. 'Scarron', ii, pp. 227–8, where the grotesque is assimilated to the burlesque).

68. E. de Goncourt, 'Préface', *EB* xxvi.

69. Cf. Gautier's Preface to Henri Monnier's *Sept Sacrements* and, on

the same artist, *La Presse*, 20 February 1855 (reprinted in *POC*). Gautier applauds Delacroix for rejecting 'la réalité photographique', *HR* 216.

70. Töpffer.

71. Gautier's Preface to Monnier's *Paris et la Province*. He returns to the attack in his Balzac essay, *SR* 168.

72. *SR* 297.

73. *RDDM*, 1 April 1841.

74. Ibid. Cf. article on Soumet's 'La Divine Epopée', *RDDM*, 1 April 1841.

75. *SR* 324–5, 329–31.

76. *Autobiographies*, Macmillan, 1955, p. 318. Cf. Pater's celebrated artistic ideal of the 'hard, gem-like flame' ('Conclusion', *Studies in the History of the Renaissance*, Macmillan, 1873, p. 210).

77. *RDDM*, 1 April 1841.

78. Ibid.

79. 'Notice', *Les Fleurs du Mal* (passage omitted from the *SR* version). Cf. Gautier: 'La plastique est l'art supérieur', cited in E. Feydeau, *Théophile Gautier. Souvenirs Intimes*, Plon, 1874, pp. 139, 144, 145–8.

80. Gautier, as reported in Houssaye's *Confessions*, v, p. 86. As always however, Gautier is generous in praising cases, like that of Lamartine, where an outstanding gift creates a law unto itself: cf. *SR* 188–98.

81. *Salon de 1845*, quoted in A. Boschot, ed., *Emaux et Camées*, op. cit, p. L.

82. 'Excellence de la Poésie', *Fusains et Eaux-Fortes*, p. 54.

83. *Caprices et Zigzags*, p. 207. The same terms are used in *Les Grotesques*, II, p. 210.

84. Cf. also *RDDM*, 1 April 1841, and 'A Cl. Popelin', 1 (*DP*).

85. Cf. Fontenelle's 'Réflexion sur la Poétique', LXX (1742), and La Faye's 'Ode en faveur du vers' (1729), strikingly foreshadowing 'L'Art', quoted in P. Van Tieghem, *Petite Histoire des Grandes Doctrines Littéraires*, *PUF*, 1957, pp. 94, 102, etc. Gautier himself often uses the term 'difficulté vaincue', e.g. *Fusains et Eaux-Fortes*, pp. 54, 212, 303, etc.

86. Gautier's obituary on J. de Goncourt, 25 June 1870, incorporated in *POC* 201.

87. J. N. Primoli affirms this to be the case, having observed Gautier at work, in 'La Princesse Mathilde et Théophile Gautier', *RDDM*, 1 and 15 November 1925. A precise example is the ingenious *trouvaille* 'singer/Clésinger', which Gautier attempted repeatedly to include in 'Le Poème de la Femme' (*EC*). Cf. *Emaux et Camées*, ed. Matoré, Droz, 1947, p. 141.

88. Phrase attributed to Flaubert and lovingly repeated by Gautier, according to the Goncourt *Journal*, *1851–1863*, Fasquelle-Flammarion, 1956, I, p. 308 (3 January 1857).

89. *HR* 344, 346–7. Cf. also article, *La Presse*, 28 July 1851, quoted at length in *PC* I, CXLIII, n. l.

90. *SR* 314–15.

91. The rediscovery of the sonnet was indeed a major achievement of the nineteenth century. Apart from Sainte-Beuve and Gautier, it was particularly used by Baudelaire, by Parnassians like Banville, Heredia and Sully Prudhomme, and by Mallarmé.

92. The *Poésies Complètes* includes over seventy sonnets, fairly evenly spread over Gautier's career, whereas the octosyllabic form is largely confined to *Emaux et Camées* (forty-three out of forty-seven poems in the definitive edition). For Gautier's identification of the sonnet with Italian gallantry, cf. *VI* 166–7.

93. E. de Goncourt's 'Préface', *EB* VII.

94. Cf. R. Giraud, 'Gautier's dehumanization of art', *L'Esprit Créateur*, III, No. 1, 1963. The Goncourts report Gautier as proclaiming 'qu'un homme ne doit se montrer affecté de rien, que cela est honteux et dégradant, qu'il ne doit jamais laisser passer de la sensibilité dans ses œuvres, que la sensibilité est un côté inférieur en art et en littérature' (*Journal*, op. cit., p. 1354, 9 November 1863).

95. *Journal Officiel*, 17 February 1870, and 'Egypte', *L'Orient*, II, p. 131.

96. *HR* 330. Cf. *EB* 72. The alleged impassivity of Goethe was legendary among Gautier's contemporaries. The identification of Gautier as the French Goethe (not seriously arguable) was commonly accepted by the poet's admirers, including Bergerat, Dierx, Feydeau and Lovenjoul.

97. *SR* 316.

98. Quoted by F. Brunot, 'La Langue française de 1815 à nos jours', in L. Petit de Julleville, *Histoire de la Langue et de la Littérature française*, A. Colin, 1899, VIII, p. 721. Cf. Banville's tribute to Gautier's command of language, *Mes Souvenirs*, Charpentier, 1882, pp. 454–5.

99. 'A un Jeune Tribun' (*CM*).

100. Quoted by Valéry in 'La Poésie et la Pensée Abstraite' (1939), *Œuvres*, Gallimard, Bibliothèque de la Pléiade, 1957, I, p. 1324.

101. Letter to E. Feydeau from St Petersburg, 16 December 1858, quoted in Feydeau, op cit., pp. 178 and 197.

102. *L'Art Moderne*, Michel Lévy, 1856, p. 60.

103. Gautier, as reported by E. de Goncourt, 'Préface', *EB* VII–VIII.

104 *Fusains et Eaux-Fortes*, p. 293.

105. *SR* 316.

106. Ibid.

107. *Caprices et Zigzags*, p. 304—an abiding stylistic ideal with Gautier. Cf. for very similar terms 'Le Bol de Punch', *Les Jeunes-France*, Charpentier, 1881, pp. 336–7. This is exactly the formula of *Le Capitaine Fracasse*, with its pastiches of the convolutions of *précieux* style.

108. *POC* 229. Cf. the magnificent and moving passage in which Gautier visualises the fusion of the arts in paradise, *Histoire de l'Art Dramatique en France*, Hetzel, 1859, III, pp. 302–3 (originally a review of Niedermeyer's opera *Marie Stuart*, 9 December 1844).

109. Cf. *L'Artiste*, 14 December 1856.

GAUTIER'S POETRY

1. Letter of 1863, quoted in Spoelberch de Lovenjoul, *Histoire des Œuvres de Théophile Gautier*, Charpentier, 1887. I, pp. 105–6.

2. H. van der Tuin, op. cit., pp. 266 ff.

3. M. C. Spencer, op. cit., pp. 3, 35–6, 100–2, etc.

4. B. L. Nicholas, 'Poetry and Pure Art', in *French Literature and its Background*, ed. J. Cruickshank, Oxford, 1969, pp. 18–19.

5. Gautier constantly reminds the reader of sources both externally (explicit titles like 'Imitation de Byron', 'Moyen Age', 'Un vers de Wordsworth', and the numerous epigraphs) and internally (allusions like 'nos auteurs chéris, Victor et Sainte-Beuve' and the lengthy enumeration of models in 'A mon ami Eugène de N***').

6. Cf. 'Préface', *Les Grotesques*. The justification of the *lieu commun* is a recurrent subject throughout *Les Grotesques*. Accepting that 'dans l'art comme dans la réalité on est toujours fils de quelqu'un' (*HR* 299), Gautier includes 'la nouveauté' in a list of non-literary virtues (cf. Barbier article, loc. cit.) and comments further: 'Shakespeare pillait ..., Molière prenait son bien partout où il le trouvait' (*Histoire de l'Art Dramatique en France*, VI, p. 267).

7. *RDDM*, 1 April 1841.

8. Cf. '*Poésies* ... is the work of a writer who ... still uses all the Gothic impedimenta of stained-glass windows, moonlit basilicas, corpses on gibbets, birds of prey, death's heads and cataracts' (J. Richardson, *Théophile Gautier*, p. 22).

9. Hazlitt, 'On Dryden and Pope', *Lectures on the English Poets*, Everyman Library, 1964, p. 72. Many analogies between Gautier and Pope could be pointed, both in detail and in general aesthetics.

10. Cf. Botticelli's celebrated painting and the billowy draperies of silken clouds ('Nonchaloir'), flowers and sea-shells ('Le Luxembourg'), zephyrs lifting undulating hair ('Les Deux Ages', 'Serment'), graceful shoulders ('Les Deux Ages'), springtime woods ('A mon ami Eugène de N***') and the poised rhythm in many poems. Gautier returns to Botticelli in 'Au Sommeil', (*CM*), while his own paintings reveal a feminine ideal similar to Botticelli's.

11. Articles of 16 and 30 November 1863 (*NL* 267, 322).

12. Cf. 'Cauchemar', 'Débauche', 'Moyen Age', 'Veillée', 'La Basilique', 'La Tête de Mort'.

13. *HR* 321.

14. Cf. *AR* 119 ff.

15. *Le Figaro*, 3 May 1834, quoted by M. Milner, *Le Diable dans la Littérature française de Cazotte à Baudelaire*, Corti, 1960, I, p. 520. According to Milner, 1830–5 was the 'Age d'or du satanisme' and it was in the Petit Cénacle that 'le genre satanique prend naissance'.

16. *Autobiographie de 1851*, in Lovenjoul, op. cit., I, XXIV, quoted in *AR* 93.

17. *SR* 9.

18. *HR* 60.

19. Apart from the mis-spelling, the quotation is misplaced from *Hamlet*, III, 2 to a non-existent III, 7. Jasinski's *PC* of 1970 still reproduces the error.

20. A. Cassagne, *La Théorie de l'Art pour l'Art en France*, Dorbon, 1906, p. 187.

21. Cf.: 'And the sad truth which hovers o'er my desk
   Turns what was once romantic to burlesque'
   (*Don Juan*, IV, iii).

22. Rabelais and Falstaff are both referred to (XI, CXII, CXVIII). The alternation of the graceful and the ponderously grotesque is a constant device in Gautier (Puck and Ariel are mentioned in XXII).

23. Article of 16 November 1863 (*NL* 275).

24. Ibid., p. 274.

25. *Dix-Neuvième Siècle: Etudes Littéraires*, Boivin, 1887, VI, p. 296.

26. *Théophile Gautier*, p. 23.

27. A. Fontainas, 'Les Poésies de Théophile Gautier', *MF*, September–October 1911.

28. The cholera epidemic of 1832 alone caused, according to some estimates, some 20,000 victims. Cf. J. Lucas-Dubreton, *La Grande Peur de 1832*, Paris, 1932.

29. *SR* 286. Cf. 'Valdès Léal', (*E*), where the Spanish painter is dubbed the 'Young de la peinture'.

30. E.g. 'La Comédie de la Mort', V: 'A tous les parias elle ouvre son auberge . . .' (an image later renewed by Baudelaire in 'La Mort des Pauvres').

31. *PC* I, XXXVII.

32. Baudelaire, article on Gautier of 13 March 1859 (*BOC* 698).

33. Cf. Jasinski's note to 'Lamento' in *PC* I, LV–LVI. The Spanish serenade is in some ways an updating of the mediaeval court ballad: cf. 'L'Echelle d'Amour', 'J'ai dans mon cœur', 'Letrilla', 'J'allais partir', and Jasinski's comments, *JE* 38, 181–2, 200–1, etc.

34. *La Presse*, 12 March 1838, quoted in *PC* I, LX–LXI. 'Lamento', 'Barcarolle' and 'Villanelle Rythmique' were all actually composed for musicians, while many other poems were subsequently set to music by various composers. Gautier enjoyed opera particularly, enthusiastically reviewing works by Cimarosa, Bellini, Donizetti, Weber, Meyerbeer, Mozart, Rossini, Verdi and, later, Wagner.

35. Berlioz, whom Gautier admired as an archetypal romantic (see his obituary notice, *Journal Officiel*, 16 March 1870, reprinted in *HR*), was on cordial terms with the poet-critic and not above begging Gautier's assistance in popularising his music: cf. Berlioz's letter to Gautier of November 1843, quoted in R. L. Evans, *Les Romantiques français et la Musique*, Champion, 1934, p. 112. Berlioz set six of Gautier's poems to music to form his song cycle 'Les Nuits d'Eté', op. 7: 'Villanelle Rythmique', 'Absence', 'Le Spectre de la Rose', the two 'Lamentos' and 'Barcarolle' (all from *CM*). The devil's 'concerto' in *A* may well recall episodes from Berlioz's *Symphonie Fantastique*, first heard in 1830.

36. Cf. Gautier's enthusiastic preview, 'Collection des Tableaux espagnols', *La Presse*, 24 September 1837.

37. Letter from Granada, 16 July 1840, quoted in *JE* 6.

38. Unpublished letter to Carlotta, quoted in *JE* 32.

39. Cf. F. Brunetière, *Histoire de la Littérature française*, Delagrave, 1921, IV, p. 228.

40. Letter to Feydeau, 11 February 1859, quoted in Feydeau, op cit., p. 187. Gautier writes that the piece 'L'Art' 'devait . . . clore le volume dont elle résume l'idée'.

41. The exceptions are the last three ('Plaintive Tourterelle', 'La Bonne Soirée', 'L'Art') and 'Préface' (only partly in octosyllabic quatrains). The use of this metre for virtually an entire volume was a striking novelty.

42. *HR* 322.

43. 'A Cl. Popelin', *DP*.

44. *Salon de 1847*, quoted in Boschot's edition of *Emaux et Camées*, p. L.

45. A. Cassagne, op. cit., p. 370. One work of this crystalline form Gautier particularly admired (cf. *HR* 301–3) was Banville's *Les Stalactites* of 1846 (cf. *Les Stalactites*, critical edition by E. Souffrin, Didier, 1942, pp. 85–6). Gautier's title may have been inspired by Charles Coran's *Onyx*, 1841, mentioned by Gautier in *HR* 297, and many affinities exist between Gautier and Coran.

46. E. Feydeau, op. cit., pp. 139, 144, 145–8. Cf. Flaubert: 'La plastique est la qualité première de l'art' ('Préface' to Bouilhet's *Dernières Chansons*, quoted by Cassagne, op. cit., p. 370).

47. Cf. H. Blaze, 'Introduction' to Goethe's *Poésies*, Charpentier, 1843: 'Goethe, interrompu dans sa contemplation éternelle par les événements

de 1811, ne trouva pas de plus sûr moyen d'y échapper que de se réfugier par la pensée en Orient' (quoted by G. Matoré, ed., *Emaux et Camées*, Droz, 1946, p. 139).

48. *HR* 322: 'Chaque pièce devait être un médaillon à enchasser sur le couvercle d'un coffret, un cachet à porter au doigt, serti dans une bague, quelque chose qui rappelât les empreintes de médailles antiques qu'on voit chez les peintres ou les sculpteurs . . .'

49. D. Parmée, *Twelve French Poets 1820–1900*, Longmans, 1962, p. 309.

50. *BOC* 684.

51. 'Préface', *Mademoiselle de Maupin*, ed. G. Matoré, Droz, 1946, p. 11.

52. Cf. *EC*, ed. M. Cottin, Minard, 1968, for precise identification of the plastic sources of each poem, with reproductions of these.

53. *La Presse*, 10 July 1843. Cf. Gautier's complete account in 'Le Club des Haschischins' (in *Romans et Contes*, Charpentier, 1880, pp. 429 ff.).

54. Cf. M. Cottin, op. cit., p. 10; and J. Seznec's review of this edition, *French Studies*, 1969, p. 421.

55. Article of 28 July 1855, reprinted in *Causeries du Lundi*, Garnier, 1857, XII, p. 5.

56. C.-A. Fusil, *Théophile Gautier, Pages Choisies*, Classiques Larousse, n.d., p. 27.

57. M. Cottin, op. cit., p. 11.

OTHER WORKS

1. 'Un Tour en Belgique et en Hollande' (in *Caprices et Zigzags*, p. 3).

2. *SR* 12.

3. E. Feydeau, op. cit., pp. 201–5.

4. *Caprices et Zigzags*, p. 1.

5. Gautier's travelling companion is usually relegated to 'mon compagnon' or 'mon camarade', and he tantalisingly remarks 'nous sommes invités à dîner en ville' or speaks of 'l'occasion d'aller à Moscou en agréable compagnie' (*VR* 91, 131) without elaborating.

6. Cf. '. . . combien l'art a dégénéré depuis ce glorieux seizième siècle, époque climatérique du monde . . .' (*VE* 329); 'le génie était dans l'air à cette époque climatérique du genre humain' (*VI* 130); and the eloquent hymn to the Parthenon in *LP* 230–1. See also above, p. 8: 'Athènes m'a transporté . . .'

7. Cf. 'leurs figures . . . ne présentaient rien de caractéristique' (*VE* 33); 'un instant nous crûmes avoir trouvé le vrai type espagnol . . . mais c'était une jeune Française' (*VE* 52). He is somewhat defensive about this comparative approach: 'Il n'est pas sans intérêt de mêler à la Venise du rêve la Venise de la réalité' (*VI* 143).

8. *Contre Sainte-Beuve*, Gallimard, Bibliothèque de la Pléiade, 1971, p. 187.

9. *EC*, Garnier, 1954, p. LVII; and cf. the same author's *Théophile Gautier*, pp. 237–8.

10. The best works on specific aspects of Gautier's criticism are H. Patch, *The Dramatic Criticism of Théophile Gautier*, Bryn Mawr, 1922; M. C. Spencer, *The Art Criticism of Théophile Gautier*, Droz, 1969; and C. Rizza, *Théophile Gautier Critico Letterario*, Turin, 1971.

11. *BOC* 677.

12. Cf. M. C. Spencer, op. cit., pp. 2–3; and see above, p. 132, n. 35.

13. E.g. P. G. Castex, *La Critique d'Art en France au XIXe Siècle*, C.D.U., 1964; A. Brookner, *The Genius of the Future, Studies in French Art Criticism*, Phaidon, 1971.

14. Cf. especially Gautier's appreciation of Gavarni's modernity (his essay in *L'Artiste* of 1855, reprinted in *POC*, anticipates Baudelaire's in *Le Présent*, October 1857); and his major contribution to the French appreciation of Goya (his article in *Le Cabinet de l'Amateur* of 1842, later included in *VE*, preceded Baudelaire's essay (1857) by fifteen years); etc.

15. Cf. M. C. Spencer, op. cit., pp. 25, 43, and J. Richardson, *Théophile Gautier*, pp. 146–8.

16. *Salon de 1846* (*BOC* 920). The question of Gautier's leniency is controversial. A. Boschot (*Théophile Gautier*, p. 253) calls his early criticism 'combatif', quoting Gautier at twenty-one finishing an article: 'le reste des tableaux est au-dessous de la critique'. Spencer agrees, and has shown generally that the early criticism (i.e. 1832–8) is more discriminating than the later. Sainte-Beuve denied that Gautier's 'indulgence' succeeds in hiding his true opinions (article on Gautier of 23 November 1863: *NL* 299–302, and article on Paul de Saint-Victor in *Nouveaux Lundis*, x, p. 442).

17. Preamble to *Salon* in *La France Industrielle*, April 1834, pp. 17–22, quoted in Spencer, op. cit., p. 94.

18. Letter to his mother, 11 August 1862 in Baudelaire, *Lettres Inédites a sa mère*, ed. J. Crépet, Conard, 1918, p. 274.

19. *BOC* 677. Gautier amusingly recalls his skirmishes with the Salon selection committees, in *HR* 232–3.

20. Articles in *La Presse*, 6 May 1851, and *L'Artiste*, 1 December 1856 respectively.

21. Cf. M. C. Spencer, op. cit., pp. 26–7.

22. *POC* 337.

23. 'Préface', *Albertus*; then *Salon* of 1833 and 'Onuphrius' in *Les Jeunes-France*, Petite Bibliothèque Charpentier, 1881, p. 82: 'nos jeunes grands maîtres, Delacroix, Ingres . . .'.

24. Cf. his article on Chardin, *Le Moniteur Universel*, 30 August 1860.

25. For detailed comment, cf. M. C. Spencer, op. cit., pp. 62–8, etc.

26. Delacroix, *Journal*, 17 June 1855.

27. Article of 30 November 1863 (*NL* 318).

28. *Chroniques Parisiennes*, 'Mai' (1887), in *Textes Inédits*, La Connaissance, n.d., p. 103.

29. *SR* 168, 119. Gautier's article dates from 1858, Baudelaire's from the following year. Gautier stresses, apart from the concept of the *voyant*, most of the qualities of Balzac since accepted as critical commonplaces.

30. Article in *La Presse*, 7 June 1852, reprinted in *HR*, and developed in 1862 in Gautier's Introduction to P. Chenay's *Dessins de Victor Hugo*, Castel, 1863 (reprinted in *Souvenirs de Théâtre, d'Art et de Critique*, Charpentier, 1883).

31. François Coppée, quoted by J. Richardson, *Théophile Gautier*, p. 290.

32. Cf. M. Dreyfous, *Ce que je tiens à dire*, Ollendorf, n.d., p. 172.

33. 'Le Petit Chien de la Marquise', in *Nouvelles*, Charpentier, 1889, p. 231.

34. 'Jean et Jeannette', in *Un Trio des Romans*, Nelson, n.d., pp. 269–70. Cf. *Guide de l'Amateur au Musée du Louvre*, p. 184: 'à cette époque, dans l'art coquet, libertin et spirituel du dix-huitième siècle, dont l'idéal était le joli . . .'

35. Gautier said of *Le Roman de la Momie*: 'Dans la *Momie*, j'ai rendu l'Egypte amusante sans rien sacrifier de l'exactitude la plus rigoureuse des détails historiques, topographiques et archéologiques' (*EB* 141). For the source of this documentation, v. E. Feydeau, op. cit., pp. 87–94.

36. 'Omphale, histoire rococo', in *Nouvelles*, p. 214.

37. For Gautier and Hoffmann—a major influence later merging with that of Poe—cf. Gautier's early articles of 1830, quoted in full in Lovenjoul, op. cit., I, pp. 11–15; and of 14 August 1836 in *La Chronique de Paris* (reprinted in *Souvenirs de Théâtre, d'Art et de Critique*). For detailed comment on Gautier's debt to Hoffmann, cf. Tuin, op. cit., pp. 158 ff; and P. G. Castex, *Le Conte fantastique en France de Nodier à Maupassant*, Corti, 1951, pp. 54–5. As for E. A. Poe, his influence is evident in 'Avatar', 'Le Pied de Momie', *Spirite*, etc. Gautier expresses admiration for Poe in the 1868 *Les Fleurs du Mal* essay (*SR* 264–5) and, through his hero Malivert, in *Spirite* (Flammarion, 1970, pp. 33–4). Cf. also J. H. Retinger, *Le Conte fantastique dans le Romantisme français*, Grasset, 1908, pp. 61, 77; and G. Poulet, *Etudes sur le Temps Humain*, Plon, 1949, I, pp. 304–6.

38. Cf. *EB* 166 ff., and Cassagne, op. cit., pp. 344–5. Balzac's *Séraphîta* impressed Gautier deeply (cf. *SR* 170–1).

39. After smoking opium in 1838 (cf. 'La Pipe d'Opium', *La Presse*, 27 September 1838), a series of works followed inspired by drugs,

notably 'Le Club des Haschischins'. Cf. R. Hughes, 'Vers la contrée du rêve: Balzac, Gautier et Baudelaire disciples de Quincey', *MF*, 1 August 1939; and G. Poulet, op. cit., 1, pp, 285–7.

40. 'La Cafetière', in *Contes Fantastiques*, Corti, 1962, pp. 18–19. His heroes Tiburce ('La Toison d'Or', in *Nouvelles*, p. 160), Octave ('Avatar', in *Romans et Contes*, p. 11), d'Albert (*MM* 131) and Malivert (*Spirite*, passim) all have very similar diagnoses.

41. Cf. G. Poulet, 'Théophile Gautier et le second *Faust*', *RLC*, January–March 1948, and *Etudes sur le Temps Humain*, 1, pp. 288–307.

42. Cf. *Spirite*, Flammarion, 1970, pp. 64–5, 134–7, 145–51. Written during the autumn of 1865 at Carlotta's Geneva estate, the novel sublimates the poet's love: 'Sous le voile d'une fiction [palpite] le vrai, le seul amour de mon cœur' (Letter to Carlotta, 17 November 1865, quoted in P. Descaves, op. cit., p. 109). The novel contains, 'de son aveu, les dix plus belles pages qu'il ait écrites' (*EB* 169).

43. E. Starkie, *From Gautier to Eliot*, Hutchinson, 1960, p. 29.

44. 'Sonnet' ('with a copy of *Mademoiselle de Maupin*'), in *Le Tombeau de Théophile Gautier*, Lemerre, 1873. Swinburne continues by describing the novel as 'an altar-fire/To the unknown God of unachieved desire'.

45. E. de Mirecourt, *Théophile Gautier*, Roret, 1855, pp. 49, 51, 53. Cf. Maxime du Camp, op. cit., p. 139.

46. Cf. *AR* 286–8.

47. M. Praz, *The Romantic Agony*, Fontana, 1966, p. 352.

48. G. Brereton, *An Introduction to the French Poets*, Methuen, 1960, p. 223.

49. Significantly, Gautier terms George Sand 'l'écrivain hermaphrodite' (*Fusains et Eaux-Fortes*, p. 52). Cf. M. Praz., op. cit., pp. 353 ff., 366, 464, etc. For Gautier and the hermaphrodite, cf. R. Giraud, 'Gautier's dehumanization of Art', *L'Esprit Créateur*, III, No. 1, 1963. In Gautier, see especially his comments on the dancer Fanny Elssler (*Le Messager*, 4 May 1838), the poem 'Contralto' (*EC*), and *MM* 99, 113, 154, 162, 189, 199, 212, 299, 320, 356, 369–70.

50. Cf. Baudelaire: 'Il y a des beautés étonnantes' (*Lettres Inédites à sa mère*, p. 302). Verlaine's admiration is recorded in P. Louÿs, *Journal*, in *Les Nouvelles Littéraires*, 16 April 1927. Proust defends *Fracasse* against Faguet's criticism in *Contre Sainte-Beuve*, Gallimard, Bibliothèque de la Pléiade, 1971, pp. 175–6, 295–6.

51. Sainte-Beuve, article of 30 November 1863 (*NL* 334). Gautier was always moved by an 'irrésistible désir rétrospectif' (*POC* 329) when faced with a great work of art: 'Qui n'a souhaité, par un désir rétrospectif, vivre un instant dans les siècles évanouis?' (*Quand on voyage*, M. Lévy, 1865, p. 313).

52. Cf. E. Feydeau, op. cit., pp. 211–12; and A. Boschot, *Théophile Gautier*, op. cit., p. 311. It was only reluctantly that Gautier was per-

suaded by his publisher Charpentier to abandon his original plan for a tragic dénouement to his novel and substitute a happy ending: cf. Judith Gautier, *RDP*, 1 January 1903, pp. 170–1.

53. Article of 30 November 1863 (*NL* 335).

54. Cf. A. Boschot's comments, *Le Capitaine Fracasse*, Garnier, 1961, pp. 503–4. A good résumé of the verbal mannerisms of the novel is given by C. Bruneau in F. Brunot, *Histoire de la Langue française*, Colin, 1953, XIII, Part 1, ch. III.

GAUTIER'S FORTUNE AND INFLUENCE

1. Article of 16 November 1863 (*NL* 274–5).
2. Quoted in *AR* 122.
3. *Les Confessions*, I, p. 306.
4. E. de Goncourt, 'Préface', *EB* VI.
5. Cf. *SR* 10, 105.
6. Cf. E. Feydeau, op. cit., p. 69.
7. Cf. J. Tild, op. cit., p. 271, and see above, p. 132, n. 35. For Gautier and Wagner, see A. Cœuroy, *Wagner et l'Esprit romantique*, Gallimard, 1965, pp. 177–87. Present at *Tannhäuser* at Wiesbaden in 1857, Gautier contributed an enthusiastic review to *Le Moniteur Universel*, 29 September 1857. His pride in promoting Wagner, 'que j'ai le premier signalé en France' is recorded by Bergerat, *EB* 156. Gautier's daughters became fervent Wagnerians, and the relationship between Wagner and Judith Gautier was for a time close and passionate.
8. P. Moreau, *Le Romantisme*, Del Duca, 1957, p. 383. Cf. R. Jasinski, *Histoire de la Littérature française*, Nizet, 1965, II, pp. 201–3, and M. Souriau, *Histoire du Parnasse*, Spes, 1929, p. 21.
9. Cf. J. Ducros, *Le Retour de la Poésie française à l'Antiquité grecque*, Colin, 1918, pp. 62–3. Bergerat records Leconte de Lisle's respect for Gautier in *Souvenirs d'un Enfant de Paris*, Charpentier, 1911–12, II, p. 154.
10. Cf. H. Dérieux, *La Plasticité de Baudelaire et ses rapports avec Gautier*, Mercure de France, 1917; E. Meyer, 'Théophile Gautier et Baudelaire', *RCC*, 15 April 1926; E. Raynaud, *Charles Baudelaire*, Garnier, 1922, pp. 310–49; J. Pommier, *Dans les Chemins de Baudelaire*, Corti, 1945; J. Prévost, *Baudelaire*, Mercure de France, 1953; R. Vivier, *L'Originalité de Baudelaire*, Bruxelles, 1965; A. Ferran, *L'Esthétique de Baudelaire*, Nizet, 1968; etc.
11. Cf. V. Fournel, *Gazette Anecdotique*, 15 January 1877, quoted in A. Albalat, *Gustave Flaubert et ses amis*, Plon, 1927, pp. 58–9; P. Berthier, 'Balzac lecteur de Gautier', *L'Année balzacienne*, Garnier, 1971, pp. 282–5; and E. Brua, 'Gautier aide de Balzac', ibid., 1972, pp. 381–4.
12. P. Martino, *Parnasse et Symbolisme*, Colin, 1950, p. 24.

13. Cf. M. du Camp, *Souvenirs littéraires*, Hachette, 1882–3, I, p. 167, and Albalat, op. cit., p. 45, quoting *Le Figaro* of 27 June 1858.

14. Cf. Houssaye, op. cit., VI, p. 96. It is worth recalling that Flaubert asked Gautier to write the libretto of an opera based on *Salammbô*, but this was never completed. Cf. Albalat, op. cit., p. 51, and Flaubert, *Correspondance*, V (1862–8), Conard, 1929, p. 118.

15. 'De l'influence de Théophile Gautier', *RDDM*, 15 July 1911.

16. Cf. E. Feydeau, op. cit., pp. 115–16.

17. Letter of J. de Goncourt, 1886, quoted in P. Sabatier, *L'Esthétique des Goncourt*, Hachette, 1920, p. 203.

18. Cf. P. Sabatier, op. cit. The stylistic fragmentation associated with *écriture artiste* was considered by Huysmans' hero, Des Esseintes, a feature of 'decadence', as also by P. Bourget in his analysis of Baudelaire's style, in *Essais de Psychologie Contemporaine*, Lemerre, 1883, I, p. 25.

19. Cf. H. Trudgian, *L'Esthétique de J.-K. Huysmans*, Conard, 1934, p. 167. See below, p. 140, n. 8.

20. Cf. J. Gengoux, *La Pensée Poétique de Rimbaud*, Nizet, 1950.

21. Cf. *L'Art*, 2 November 1865. In *Mémoires d'un Veuf*, Verlaine speaks warmly of *Mademoiselle de Maupin*, *Emaux et Camées* and 'Ténèbres' (*Œuvres Compl.*, Messein, 1926, IV, p. 258). Cf. also his review of Hugo's 'Paris' (*Œuvres Posths.*, Messein, 1922–9, II, p. 318). The 'Prologue' and 'Epilogue' of *Poèmes Saturniens* unmistakably reflect Gautier's views. See also above, p. 136, n. 50.

22. Cf. G. Zayed, *La Formation littéraire de Verlaine*, Nizet, 1970, pp. 308–10, 396–7.

23. Undated letter (1873) to Coppée, referring to his contribution to *Le Tombeau de Théophile Gautier*: 'Je chanterai le voyant qui, placé dans ce monde, l'a regardé, ce qu'on ne fait pas' (Mallarmé, *Œuvres Complètes*, Gallimard, Bibliothèque de la Pléiade, 1945, p. 1470). Cf. A. R. Chisholm, *Mallarmé's Grand Œuvre*, Manchester University Press, 1962, p. 61; and L. Cellier, *Mallarmé et la Morte qui parle*, PUF, 1959, ch. IV.

24. Cf. G. Michaud, *Mallarmé*, Hatier-Boivin, 1953, p. 13, and A. Thibaudet, *La Poésie de Stéphane Mallarmé*, NRF, 1926, p. 274.

25. Cf. L. J. Austin, 'Mallarmé and Gautier: new light on *Toast Funèbre*', in *Balzac and the 19th Century. Studies in French Literature presented to H. J. Hunt*, Leicester University Press, 1972.

26. Cf. J. C. Ireson, 'Towards a theory of the Symbolist theatre', in *Studies in French Literature presented to H. W. Lawton*, Manchester University Press, 1968.

27. Besides evident general affinities between Gautier and Valéry, J. Pommier has noted, for example, a precise echo of 'La Comédie de la Mort' in 'Le Cimetière Marin' (cf. *Dans les Chemins de Baudelaire,*

p. 195). For Valéry's early admiration for Gautier, cf. the letter of Fourment, September 1889, in *Paul Valéry—G. Fourment: Correspondance, 1887–1933*, Gallimard, 1957, pp. 72–3.

28. See the respective essays on each in *HR* and *SR*. Gautier also uses the term *voyant* in 'Le Club des Haschischins' and twice in *Spirite* (Flammarion, 1970, pp. 139, 189).

29. *The Heritage of Symbolism*, Macmillan, 1943, pp. 3, 6.

30. C. Spoelberch de Lovenjoul, *Histoire des Œuvres de Théophile Gautier*, 2 vols., Charpentier, 1887; and cf. also the same author's *Les Lundis d'un Chercheur*, Calmann Lévy, 1894.

31. Letter to E. Stedman, 23 February 1874 (*The Letters of A. C. Swinburne*, ed. Cecil Y. Lang, Yale University Press 1959, II, p. 281). See E. Starkie, *From Gautier to Eliot*, Hutchinson, 1960, for a general survey of Gautier's influence on English literature, and, for the specific case of Swinburne and Gautier, G. Lafourcade, *La Jeunesse de Swinburne, 1837–1867*, Les Belles Lettres, 2 vols., 1928, II, pp. 81, 337–40, 370–2.

32. 'Notes on some Pictures of 1868', in *Essays and Studies*, Chatto & Windus, 1875, p. 375.

33. Ibid.

34. Swinburne's 'The Hermaphrodite' (based on the same Louvre statue) is adapted from Gautier's 'Contralto' (*EC*), 'Love at Sea' is 'imitated from Gautier' ('Barcarolle', *CM*), etc. Cf. E. Starkie, op. cit., pp. 43–6 and P. de Reul, *L'Œuvre de Swinburne*, Robert Sand, 1922, pp. 190, 247.

35. E. Legouis and L. Cazamian, *History of English Literature*, Dent, 1948, p. 1259. Cf. the standard works on the subject: A. J. Farmer, *Le Mouvement esthétique et 'décadent' en Angleterre (1873–1900)*, Champion, 1931; and L. Rosenblatt, *L'Idée de l'Art pour l'art dans la Littérature anglaise pendant la période victorienne*, Champion, 1931.

36. Payne (1842–1916) was already a fervent francophile by 1873 when, with Swinburne, he contributed to *Le Tombeau de Théophile Gautier*. He translated almost fifty of Gautier's poems, included in *Flowers of France: the Romantic Period*, Villon Society, I, 1906.

37. *Confessions of a Young Man*, Heinemann, 1926, pp. 53–4 (first published in France in *La Revue Indépendante*, 1886).

38. Many passages in *Dorian Gray* alone read as direct paraphrases of Gautier, while Gautier's name recurs several times in the novel (Penguin Modern Classics, 1971, pp. 124, 144, 181–3, etc.). *Dorian Gray* is also indebted to Huysmans, as Huysmans was to Gautier.

39. Cf. R. Taupin, *L'Influence du Symbolisme français sur la Poésie américaine de 1910 à 1920*, Champion, 1929.

40. F. S. Flint, 'History of Imagism', *Egoist*, 1 May 1915.

41. Cf. the letter of 1928 to René Taupin, quoted in D. Davie,

Ezra Pound, Poet as Sculptor, Routledge, 1965, p. 178; and E. Pound 'The Hard and Soft in French Poetry', in *Literary Essays of Ezra Pound*, Faber, 1968, pp. 285–9.

42. *Egoist*, April 1918.

43. Cf. E. J. H. Greene, *T. S. Eliot et la France*, Boivin, 1951; F. Scarfe, 'Eliot and 19th century French poetry', in *Eliot in Perspective*, ed. C. G. Martin, Macmillan, 1970; and R. Taupin, op. cit., pp. 238–9.

44. E. Pound, 'Harold Munro', *The Criterion*, xi, October 1931–July 1932; and 'The Hard and Soft in French Poetry', op. cit. Cf. Taupin, op. cit., p. 59: around 1917, 'Gautier sauva la poésie [américaine] d'une nouvelle crise d'abandon et de facilité'. See also Davie, op. cit., p. 98.

45. D. Davie, op. cit., pp. 94, 99, 101.

CRITICAL EVALUATION

1. *PC* i, lxxi.

2. 'Symphonie littéraire', in Mallarmé, *Œuvres Complètes*, Gallimard, Bibliothèque de la Pléiade, 1945, p. 261.

3. Essay, 'The Hard and Soft in French Poetry', op. cit. Cf. Gautier's expressed indifference to subject-matter in painting (see above, p. 79) and literature (ibid., pp. 19, 98).

4. 'Les Chants Modernes', in *Causeries du Lundi*, Garnier, 1857, xii, p. 5.

5. 'Théophile Gautier', lecture delivered at the Vieux-Colombier theatre, April 1914, reprinted in *Incidences*, Gallimard, 1924, p. 155. In his 'Préface' to *Les Fleurs du Mal* (Pelletan, 1917), Gide terms Gautier 'l'artisan le plus sec, le moins musicien, le moins méditatif que notre littérature ait produit' (*Incidences*, p. 159), and in 1921, 'un des plus inutiles péroreurs dont puisse s'encombrer une littérature' (*Journal*, 1889–1939, Gallimard, Bibliothèque de la Pléiade, 1951, p. 714).

6. H. van der Tuin, op. cit., pp. 126–7.

7. 'Préface', *EB* iii. Cf. *L'Artiste*, 5 September 1858: 'Nous sommes sur la limite d'un monde qui finit . . .'

8. It is significant that Moreau was later the favourite painter of Huysmans' decadent hero Des Esseintes in *A Rebours*, (1884), and also that Des Esseintes was long an admirer of Gautier (cf. *A Rebours*, Charpentier, 1923, ch. xiv, p. 215). For Gautier's influence on Huysmans, cf. H. Trudgian, *L'Esthétique de J.-K. Huysmans*, Conard, 1934, and M. E. Drougard's notes on the relationship of 'Fortunio' to *A Rebours*, *MF*, 1 October 1931, pp. 211 ff.

9. For discussion of the theme in relation to a single work, cf. A. Bouchard, 'Le masque et le miroir dans *Mademoiselle de Maupin*', *RHLF*,

July–August 1972. See also L. Cellier, *Mallarmé et la Morte qui parle*, chs. IV and V.

10. Article of 9 December 1844, reprinted in *Histoire de l'Art Dramatique en France*, Hetzel, 1859, III, pp. 302–3.

11. Cf. M. Crouzet, 'Gautier et le problème de créer', *RHLF*, July–August 1972.

12. Funeral oration on Gautier, reprinted in *EB* 236.

13. Letter to E. Feydeau from St Petersburg, 7 February 1859.

14. Quoted in Sainte-Beuve, *Nouveaux Lundis*, XIV, p. 73.

15. Mallarmé, undated letter (1873) to Coppée, quoted in Mallarmé, *Œuvres Complètes*, Gallimard, Bibliothèque de la Pléiade, 1945, p. 1470.

16. Cf. Gautier's mouthpiece, Don Juan, searching for an ideal feminine type 'réunissant Cléopâtre et Marie' ('La Comédie de la Mort', VII).

17. Cf. the devil's criticism of creation as a decorative failure in *Une Larme du Diable*, *Théâtre*, Charpentier, 1882, p. 26.

18. Cf. *MM* 83, 149, 151, 203, 252; and 'Le Triomphe de Pétrarque' (*CM*); etc.

19. *L'Art Moderne*, Michel Lévy, 1856, p. 60. Cf. M. Eigeldinger, 'L'Image solaire dans la poésie de Gautier', *RHLF*, July–August 1972, and the same author's introduction to *Spirite*, Nizet, 1970.

20. Cf., for the similar case of Banville, E. Souffrin, 'Banville et la Poétique du Décor, in *French Nineteenth Century Painting and Literature*, ed. U. Finke, Manchester University Press, 1972.

21. Cf. Gautier's 'Notice' to *Les Fleurs du Mal* on the 'dialecte racinien' (*SR* 287) and 'Préface', *EB* VIII–IX.

22. For the verbal exuberance of the *bousingot*, cf. the education of Daniel Jovard in *Les Jeunes-France*: 'Il lui ouvrit un vaste répertoire de formules admiratives et réprobatives: phosphorescent, transcendental, pyramidal, stupéfiant, foudroyant, annihilant, et mille autres...' (Petite Bibliothèque Charpentier, 1881, p. 136); and the analysis of verbal pyrotechnics, ibid., pp. 336–7. See G. Matoré, *Le Vocabulaire et la Société sous Louis-Philippe*, Droz, 1951, pp. 72 ff., for detailed analysis.

23. C.-E. Magny, *Précieux Giraudoux*, Seuil, 1945, pp. 23 ff.

24. Tuin, op. cit., p. 274. Tuin further calls the octosyllabic form 'stoïque', 'plus statique que dynamique'.

25. Article on *Les Fausses Confidences*, *Le Moniteur Universel*, 10 October 1855. Gautier's defence of Marivaux is one of the positive features of his dramatic criticism. Marivaux is for Gautier 'le subtil, l'ingénieux, le délicat' (*Histoire de l'Art Dramatique*, VI, pp. 217–18). Moreover, Marivaux's self-defence against attacks on his *préciosité* (cf. *Le Spectateur français*, VIII, 8 September 1722) is similar to Gautier's defence—and also to Gautier's defence of Baudelaire's 'maniérisme' (*SR* 284). Cf. also

NL 301–2. Gautier's own 'théâtre idéal' in *MM* 242 ff. may usefully be set beside his appreciations of Marivaux, and also his own theatre.

26. F. Deloffre, *Une Préciosité Nouvelle: Marivaux et le Marivaudage*, Colin, 1967.

27. For Gautier and Ronsard, cf. *HR* 304, 345; *POC* 204; *MM* 186. Cf. Ronsard's 'Art Poétique' and the 'Odes' to Gaspar d'Auvergne, Bonjou and Pisseleu, etc.

28. *Poésies* especially contains a significant incidence of epigraphs from sixteenth-century and earlier courtly poets. Cf. L. Nicolardot's comments, *L'Impeccable Théophile Gautier*, Tresse, 1883, and the critical edition of *Poésies* (1830) by H. Cockerham, Athlone Press, 1973.

29. Besides *Le Capitaine Fracasse* (see above, p. 90), cf. 'L'Hirondelle' (*DP*), imitated from Marot, 'La Demoiselle' (*P*), modelled on Belleau's 'Avril', etc.

30. Cf. R. Bray, *La Préciosité et les Précieux de Thibaut de Champagne à Jean Giraudoux*, Nizet, 1948.

31. Cf. *Poésies* ('Serment', 'La Demoiselle', 'Promenade Nocturne'); *España* ('L'Horloge', 'Au Bord de la Mer', 'J'ai laissé de mon sein de neige', 'Le Laurier du Généralife'); *La Comédie de la Mort* ('Les Papillons', 'Rocaille', 'Tombée du Jour', 'Le Spectre de la Rose', 'Barcarolle', 'Pour veiner de son front', 'A deux beaux yeux'); *Dernières Poésies* ('La Neige', 'Le Rose', 'L'Hirondelle', the Mathilde cycle); etc. Cf. P. E. Tennant, 'Preciosity in the Poetry of Théophile Gautier', unpublished thesis, University of Reading, 1971.

32. J. Debû-Bridel, 'La préciosité conception héroïque', *RDF*, 15 September 1938.

33. C.-E. Magny, op. cit., pp. 40 ff.

34. Article on Hugo's *Les Burgraves*, *La Presse*, 13–14 March 1843.

35. Cf. G. Poulet, 'Théophile Gautier et le second *Faust*', *RLC*, January–March 1948; and *Etudes sur le Temps Humain*, Plon, 1949, I, pp. 288–307.

36. *La Presse*, September 1851, and *L'Orient*, I, p. 352.

37. *Guide de l'Amateur au Musée du Louvre*, p. 222.

38. Cf. *La Presse*, 10 July 1843, republished as 'Le Club des Haschi-schins' in 1846.

39. *Histoire de l'Art dramatique*, v, p. 285.

40. Letter to L. d'Orfer, 27 June 1884, reprinted in *La Vogue*, 1886.

41. Lecture given at the Vieux-Colombier theatre, April 1914, reprinted in *Incidences*, Gallimard, 1924, p. 155.

42. *Spirite*, Flammarion, 1970, p. 150.

SELECT BIBLIOGRAPHY

EDITIONS

G. van den Bogaert, *Mademoiselle de Maupin*, Garnier-Flammarion, 1966.

G. van den Bogaert, *Le Roman de la Momie*, Garnier-Flammarion, 1966.

G. van den Bogaert, *Le Capitaine Fracasse*, Garnier-Flammarian, 1967.

A. Boschot, *Emaux et Camées* (suivis de *Poésies Choisies*), Garnier, 1954.

A. Boschot, *Théophile Gautier: Souvenirs Romantiques*, Garnier, 1929.

H. Cockerham, *Poésies* (1830), Critical edition, 'Athlone French Poets', Athlone Press, 1973.

M. Cottin, *Emaux et Camées*, Minard, 1968.

P. Descaves, *Les Plus Belles Lettres de Théophile Gautier*, Calmann-Lévy, 1962.

M. Eigeldinger, *Spirite*, Nizet, 1970.

R. Jasinski, *Les Jeunes-France*, 'Nouvelle bibliothèque romantique', Flammarion, 1974.

R. Jasinski, *L' 'España' de Th. Gautier*, Edition Critique, Vuibert, 1929.

R. Jasinski, *Théophile Gautier. Poésies Complètes*, 3 vols., Nizet, 1970.

G. Matoré, *La Préface de Mademoiselle de Maupin*, Edition critique, Droz, 1946.

J. Pommier et G. Matoré, *Emaux et Camées*, Droz, 1947.

CRITICISM

P. Albouy, 'Le Mythe de l'Androgyne dans "Mademoiselle de Maupin" ', *RHLF*, July–August 1972.

X. Aubryet, *Chez nous et chez nos voisins: Théophile Gautier spiritualiste*, Dentu, 1878.

C. Baudelaire, Articles 'Théophile Gautier', *'L'Artiste*, 13 March 1859, and *Revue fantaisiste*, 15 July 1861, both reprinted in *L'Art Romantique*, 1869. See Baudelaire, *Œuvres Complètes*, Gallimard, Bibliothèque de la Pléiade, 1961.

H. Bédarida, *Théophile Gautier et l'Italie*, Boivin, 1934.

R. Benesch, *Le Regard de Théophile Gautier*, Zurich, 1969.

E. Bergerat, *Théophile Gautier: Entretiens, souvenirs et correspondance*, Charpentier, 1879.

P. Bernard, 'Théophile Gautier', *Etudes*, 5 and 20 February, 5 March, 5 May and 5 June 1912.

E. Binney, *Les Ballets de Théophile Gautier*, Nizet, 1965.

C. Book-Senninger, *Théophile Gautier auteur dramatique*, Nizet, 1972.

A. Boschot, *Théophile Gautier*, Desclée de Brouwer, 1933.

A. Bouchard, 'Le masque et le miroir dans "Mademoiselle de Maupin" ', *RHLF*, July–August 1972.

M. Breuillac, 'Hoffmann en France', *RHLF*, July–September 1906.

C. Bruneau, *Explication de Théophile Gautier: Emaux et Camées*, Centre de Documentation Universitaire, n.d. (1939).

C. Bruneau, *Histoire de la Langue française, des Origines à nos jours* (ed. F. Brunot), vols. xii and xiii, A. Colin, 1948, 1953.

G. Brunet, 'Théophile Gautier poète', *MF*, 15 October 1922.

R. Canat, *Une forme du Mal du Siècle: Du sentiment de la solitude morale chez les romantiques et les parnassiens*, Hachette, 1904.

A. E. Carter, *The Idea of Decadence in French literature, 1830–1900*, University of Toronto Press, 1958.

A. Cassagne, *La Théorie de l'Art pour l'art en France chez les derniers romantiques et les premiers réalistes*, Lucien Dorbon, 1906 (reprinted 1959).

P.-G. Castex, *Le Conte fantastique en France de Nodier à Maupassant*, Corti, 1951.

P.-G. Castex, 'Gautier aujourd'hui', *Les Nouvelles Littéraires*, 6–12 November 1972.

L. Cellier, *Mallarmé et la morte qui parle*, PUF, 1959.

L. Cellier, 'Gautier, un écrivain d'avenir', *Les Nouvelles Littéraires*, 6–12 November 1972.

L. Cellier, 'Présentation' [of Gautier], *RHLF*, July–August 1972.

R. Chambers, 'Gautier et le complexe de Pygmalion', *RHLF*, July–August 1972.

J. Charpentier, 'La réaction parnassienne et le renouveau de la fantaisie', *MF*, 15 March 1925.

A. Crampon, 'Les Fantaisistes', *RDDM*, November 1852.

M. Crouzet, 'Gautier et le problème de "créer" ', *RHLF*, July–August 1972.

B. Delvaille, *Théophile Gautier*, Seghers, 1968.

L. B. Dillingham, *The Creative Imagination of Théophile Gautier*, Princeton, 1927 (Psychological Monographs, vol. 37).

M. Du Camp, *Théophile Gautier*, Hachette, n.d. (1919).

M. Easton, *Artists and Writers in Paris: the Bohemian Idea, 1803–1867*, Arnold, 1964.

M. Eigeldinger, 'L'Image solaire dans la poésie de Théophile Gautier', *RHLF*, July–August 1972.

E. Feydeau, *Théophile Gautier, souvenirs intimes*, Plon, 1874.

A. Fontainas, 'Les Poésies de Théophile Gautier', *MF*, 16 September 1911.

J. Gautier, *Le Collier des Jours*, Juven, 1907.

J. Gautier, *Le Second Rang du Collier*, Juven, 1909.

A. J. George, 'Théophile Gautier and the romantic short story', *L'Esprit Créateur*, Spring, 1963.

R. Giraud, 'Gautier's dehumanization of Art', *L'Esprit Créateur*, Spring, 1963.

E. and J. de Goncourt, *Journal*, Charpentier, 1887–96.

E. de Goncourt, 'Préface' to E. Bergerat (q.v.).

E. Henriot, 'Théophile Gautier poète', *Les Annales Romantiques*, July–August 1912.

A. Houssaye, *Les Confessions. Souvenirs d'un demi-siècle littéraire, 1830–90*, Dentu, 1885–91.

R. Hughes, 'Vers la Contrée du Rêve: Balzac, Gautier et Baudelaire disciples de Quincey', *MF*, August 1939.

R. Jasinski, *Les Années Romantiques de Th. Gautier*, Vuibert, 1929.

C. Spoelberch de Lovenjoul, *Histoire des Œuvres de Théophile Gautier*, 2 vols., Charpentier, 1887.

R. G. Mahieu, 'Le Théâtre de Théophile Gautier', *PMLA*, vol. 53, March 1938.

H. Marcel, *Essai sur Théophile Gautier*, Société d'éditions littéraires et artistiques, Ollendorff, 1903.

G. Matoré, *Le Vocabulaire et la Société sous Louis-Philippe*, Droz, 1951.

L. Nicolardot, *L'Impeccable Théophile Gautier et les sacrilèges romantiques*, Tresse, 1883.

A. Orliac, 'Essai sur le pessimisme chez les parnassiens', *MF*, 15 August 1928.

H. Patch, *The Dramatic Criticism of Théophile Gautier*, Bryn Mawr, 1922.

J. Pommier, *Dans les Chemins de Baudelaire*, Corti, 1945.

H. Potez, *Théophile Gautier*, A. Colin, 1903.

G. Poulet, *Etudes sur le Temps Humain*, I, Plon, 1949.

G. Poulet, *Trois Essais de Mythologie romantique*, Corti, 1966.

J. N. Primoli, 'La Princesse Mathilde et Théophile Gautier', *RDDM*, 1 and 15 November 1925.

J. Richardson, *Théophile Gautier, his Life and Times*, Reinhardt, 1958.

J. Richer, 'Portrait de l'artiste en nécromant', *RHLF*, July–August 1972.

M. Riffaterre, 'Rêve et réalité dans l'*Italia* de Théophile Gautier', *L'Esprit Créateur*, Spring, 1963.

C. Rizza, *Théophile Gautier Critico Letterario*, University of Turin, Filologia Moderna, vol. VI, 1971.

C. A. Sainte-Beuve, Articles of 16, 23 and 30 November 1863 (*Nouveaux Lundis*, Michel Lévy, 1875, VI).

M. Schneider, *La littérature fantastique en France*, Fayard, 1964.

M. Schneider, '*Mademoiselle de Maupin*: la contestation sans agressivité politique', *Les Nouvelles Littéraires*, 6–12 November 1972.

S. O. Simches, *Le romantisme et le goût esthétique du XVIIIe siècle*, PUF, 1964.

A. B. Smith, *Ideal and Reality in the fictional narratives of Théophile Gautier*, University of Florida Press, 1969.

J. M. Smith, 'Gautier man of paradox', *L'Esprit Créateur*, Spring, 1963.

E. Souffrin, 'Banville et la Poétique du Décor', in *French Nineteenth Century Painting and Literature*, ed. U. Finke, Manchester University Press, 1972.

M. Souriau, *Histoire du Parnasse*, Spes, 1929.

M. C. Spencer, *The Art Criticism of Théophile Gautier*, Droz, 1969.

M. Spronck, *Les artistes littéraires: études sur le XIXe siècle*, Calmann-Lévy, 1889.

J. Tild, *Théophile Gautier et ses amis*, Albin Michel, 1951.

H. van der Tuin, *L'Evolution psychologique, esthétique et littéraire de Théophile Gautier*, Amsterdam, 1933.

E. de Ullmann, 'L'art de la transposition dans la poésie de Théophile Gautier', *Le Français Moderne*, vol. 15, 1947.

H. E. A. Velthuis, *Théophile Gautier. L'Homme, l'Artiste*, Groningen, 1924.

J. Wilcox, 'The beginnings of Art for Art's Sake', *Journal of Aesthetics*, XI, 1953.

C. Yriarte, *Les Portraits Cosmopolites*, Lachaud, 1870.

GENERAL INDEX

INDEX OF CHARACTERS AND WORKS